I'm Fine

I'm Fine

Simone Forrester

First paperback edition 2023

Book design by PublishingPush

978-1-80541-213-7 (paperback)
978-1-80541-212-0 (ebook)

Dedication

I would like to dedicate this book to my sister; my absolute rock and my constant throughout this whole shit show. I love you so much.

I'd love to dedicate the book to my husband as well. Without you dying on me, I would never have written this. I wish I could shout your name from the rooftops as I am so proud to be your wife but I can't divulge your name without upsetting a lot of people.

My sister really wanted me to write this in my real name. She was hell-bent on me making an appearance on *This Morning*. Unfortunately, as the shit in this book is real and has really happened, if I swan on to greet Phil and Holly some of the people referred to in this will have an apoplexy, so I shall remain mysterious and incognito as Simone!

December 2019

Jake's operation is tomorrow.

I don't really want to go to work, but maybe it will keep me distracted. I have a short walk into the office, about fifteen minutes. On my way in, I see a magpie. I panic as only seeing one is supposed to be unlucky. I'm looking around for another but don't spot one. Then, a single white feather falls in front of me. I stop and look around and can't see where it came from plus the single magpie has disappeared.

A few minutes on, I spot a black circle of beads on the pavement. On closer inspection, I see it is actually a rosary bracelet.

By the time I get to work, I haven't worked out whether these are good or bad omens to see before the operation.

At work, I pretty much fuck up everything I touch and my boss sends me home, mainly because I'm a liability today. Although I'm trying not to show it, I'm so scared about tomorrow.

Home by lunchtime and Jake's not that impressed. He

doesn't need my angst to deal with and I can see he's trying to hold it together for me.

Our mate Greg picks us up to take us to the glamorous Travelodge we're staying overnight in as the op is scheduled for stupid o'clock tomorrow.

I try to persuade Jake to have dinner at a nice gastropub in the town where the hospital is located, but it is pissing down and blowing a gale. So, instead, we decide on the carvery, which is attached to the hotel. Anyone who knows Jake and I knows we are massive foodies so this is unchartered territory!

We walk into said carvery with smells of overcooked veg. We are seated quickly despite how busy it is. It's full of parents and kids. I suppose it's because it's so early.

We order two diet cokes. Jake is not allowed to drink alcohol before the op tomorrow. I am taking one for the team so red wine is off the menu. Do not think I could deal with the daggers he would give me if I had wine, but bloody hell, I'd love a glass.

Did not know it even existed but they do a 'platter'. Okay, so it isn't a Spanish tapas or charcuterie board, but it does have pigs in blankets, roast parsnips, garlic bread and a dipping sauce of gravy. FFS!

It's not horrendous and, to be honest with you, we're both trying to just kill time until the morning.

We go back to the room about 8 p.m. We both need an early night.

I can feel him tossing and turning in the night. I just lay there waiting for the morning to come.

***

11/12/2019 Operation Day

Neither Jake nor I drive, so we walk to the hospital. It's only about fifteen minutes away and we need to be there by 7:30 a.m.

Once we get to the hospital, we find where we're supposed to be. It's a pre-op waiting room and we check in. The woman behind the desk is nuts.

She is wittering on about her printer and having a good old chat to herself. She checks us in and shows us where to wait. There's another couple waiting, bit older than us (well, me at least), and Jake strikes up a conversation. They tell us the husband is in for an op for his aneurysm too.

This chap is having open surgery and Jake's is keyhole. So, on the face of it, it seems less complicated (if only I fucking knew).

The other couple both seem nervous as well; the wife says she is leaving the hospital as soon as her husband goes down for his op as she cannot bear waiting around worrying.

Jake and this other chap start discussing the size of their aneurysms. It's a bit like *Jaws* with the scars. Jake wins as his aneurysm is bigger. Think he is secretly pleased.

The anaesthetist comes to take Jake for his pre-op.

When he comes back after about fifteen minutes, he is out of his civvies and in his dressing gown and slippers. I look at him and he looks so vulnerable but I know we need to do this.

Jake's consultant Mr C isn't performing the operation. Funny enough, Mr C is scheduled to do the operation for the other patient we were talking to.

Jake has the head surgeon Mr G doing his operation. He turns up to have a little chat with us. He tells Jake that, on a scale of high risk to low risk, Jake's operation is about mid risk. I think that is supposed to be reassuring.

Mr G lets me know the operation should take approximately four hours and I shouldn't expect to hear anything before lunchtime. He reassures me that as soon as Jake is in recovery, they will call me.

I don't regret too much throughout my life but I do regret not holding him a little longer or a little tighter before we said goodbye and he went down for the operation.

I told him he would be okay but looking at his face, I think he was more worried about how I would get through the next few hours.

As they're wheeling him down the corridor, the crazy arsed woman who checked us in turns to me and holds two fingers up to me. I assume she was indicating that the op will only take a couple of hours. Sweet, I think. However, in hindsight, maybe she was giving me the two finger salute?

I go down to the little coffee shop to wait for my company for the day. Two of Jake's sisters are coming to keep me company in shifts.

Liz turns up about 9ish.

Endless cups of coffee are consumed and we talk about shit in general. I can't remember if we even spoke about the op. It was just a waiting game. I was grateful for the company.

Rachel turns up at lunchtime. They swap shifts, mainly to stop them from killing each other. You know how big families are.

Rachel turns into my mother trying to force-feed me satsumas and strawberries which I refuse. I have no appetite at all. This is extremely unusual. I do manage to force down a dark KitKat from the extortionate coffee shop.

It is now past 2 p.m. Rachel is trying to encourage me to chase up what is going on. Maybe it's because I am chicken shit or something but I feel they do not need a neurotic wife harassing them, so for an hour, I put it off.

It's now 3 p.m. Shit. Now I am feeling sick. I call the ward where he was due to be discharged to once he was in recovery. He is not there yet. They say they will call me ASAP but not to worry, it is quite normal and the op could take up to eight hours.

Rachel and I sit outside a room along a corridor just to get some peace as everywhere is so busy. We sit there for hours (I think).

We decide to go to the ward to speak to someone as it's now gone 5 p.m.

I speak to the nurse at the desk. She checks her records and says he's not there but tells me Jake's in the main X-ray department. I ask why that would be and she tells me that maybe it's because there aren't enough beds at the moment. This makes me feel a little better.

We go down to main X-ray and I speak to another nurse. From the moment I tell her who I am, I know something is very wrong. I can feel this whooshing inside my head.

She tells me to take a seat (which incidentally is in a corner of an archiving cupboard) and brings me a coffee. She tells me Mr C (Jake's consultant) is coming to see me. This is not good as he was not doing the op. He was doing the other dude's operation which has clearly fucking finished.

The minute I see Mr C's face, I know my life is about to implode. He tells me of all the issues that have occurred during the op. Mr C has been observing the operation for a couple of hours since Jake started to deteriorate. He says Jake's kidneys are failing and he is in a critical condition.

I tell Mr C that I'll give Jake my kidney. He puts his hand on my knee and tells me they'll get Jake up to ICU and wired up to a dialysis machine, get him stable and then we can talk.

Mr C looks distraught himself which is even more unnerving. Jake was under his care up to the operation and he was always very straight talking. I didn't feel he had a particularly great bedside manner, but Jake really liked that about him. The fact he is being very kind is scaring the absolute fuck out of me.

Do you know where Rachel and I were sitting all that time? Outside where my Jake was. We didn't know. How would we have known? It's like fucking fate. If only I knew.

I still haven't seen Jake. Me and Rachel make our way up to ICU. They take us into the 'family room' telling us it will be more comfortable for us. Usually, you just sit in this shitty waiting room, but this room has an ensuite toilet.

I know that us being in there means more than they are letting on. It is completely private.

A couple of nurses come in to talk to me. It's been about forty-five minutes since I have spoken with Jake's consultant. I just want to see Jake.

The surgeon comes in with his entourage and tells me Jake is gravely ill and one of the other members of the surgical team nudges Mr G and says, 'Tell her about his legs.' They tell me they think Jake may be paralysed. Holy fuck, my guts drop out of my arse. This can't be fucking happening. I ask to see him.

Finally, I go. Jesus, he's writhing in pain. He is only semi-conscious and I don't know if he can see or hear me. There are wires everywhere and nurses attaching him to machinery. They're still trying to attach him to the dialysis machine. Why is it taking so long?

Jake's eyes are closed. He starts to retch. I am worried as he is flat on his back. I indicate this to the nurse and she tries to sit him up. She gives me a paper bowl in case he's sick. Then they jab him with something. I just think, *Please God, let it knock him out*. I can't bear it. He's got this residue all round his lips like he's seriously thirsty. It's utterly heartbreaking.

I hold on to his hand and I stroke his head. I tell him I am here but I really don't think he can hear me. I tell him to hang on and that he will be okay but that he needs to fight. Please fight, Jake.

The nurses ask me to leave as they still have a lot to do to stabilise him.

I go back into the family room and minutes or hours later, fuck knows, the doctors come back in. There's so many of them and they tell me I need to contact the rest of the family. Jake's sister takes over.

From this moment, the timescales are blurred.

I remember Jake's two daughters turning up; his brother and nieces as well. They all go in and see him. In typical Forrester family style, we try to make light of it. We are an inappropriate family full of wrongness that in any other scenario would be okay. But I can't take it and eventually I sit myself outside of the room down the corridor with my head in my hands.

Jake's brother tries to get hold of Jake's son.

Through Bob, I am told that Jake's son says it's too close to when his nan died so he doesn't think he can handle it. I literally want to strangle the fucker. It's his father, he should be here. I offer to pay for an Uber for him so he can get here quickly.

I go back to sitting outside the room down the corridor. Could murder a fag, but I gave up three years ago.

12/12/19 Midnight

I go back into the family room. A nurse comes in and explains to me that Jake has gone into cardiac arrest and they are trying to resuscitate him. She asks me if I want to come and witness it.

I say yes. Rachel asks if I want her to come in too. For some reason, I shout, 'No.'

Nothing prepares you for the sight of seeing someone, anyone, being resuscitated. He looks so small. There's someone on his chest doing compressions. There are machines buzzing everywhere and about ten other doctors and nurses. I can't handle it; I know I'm going to collapse.

The nurse gets me a chair but I just can't watch anymore. So, she takes me back to the family room.

Time passes by. I'm not sure how long I have been

sitting here for, but then the doctors and nurses come back in and say they're sorry but he's gone.

I sit on the floor and I don't remember anyone else being there. I just remember this female doctor who put her arms round me and let me weep and weep.

Times passes, I remember Jake's brother saying he'll call Jake's son and also Jake's other siblings and for that I am grateful.

I look at my phone and see messages of good wishes and people asking how Jake's got on and I just don't know what to do.

A nurse comes in and asks if I want to see Jake. I do, so I go into ICU and there is a privacy curtain around his bed. It's cliché but he looks like he's asleep.

The nurse gives me a little booklet and tells me how sorry she is and says tomorrow I need to call the bereavement line and they'll go through what happens next. She says it's all in this booklet but I'm not really listening. I'm just looking at Jake.

She leaves me alone and I grab a chair and sit as close to him as I can. I almost try to physically get into the bed but I don't think I'd fit. So, I just hold his hand and kiss his little fuzzy head.

After a while, Bob comes in and he sits on the other side of Jake. There's a kind of sighing noise and we both look at each other. Has Jake just taken a breath? But then we both realise it's just one of the machines making the noise. For a split second, I thought he had come back.

I stay with Jake for as long as I can until I see his lips are just starting to pale and then I leave him.

Rachel tells me I need to call my sister and parents.

I go into the corridor away from everyone. I try my sister but there's no answer and I realise it's gone midnight. I call my mum and dad and Mum just screams down the phone when I tell her he didn't make it. I tell her she has to be strong for me and say I'll call her tomorrow.

I speak to my sister. She's shell shocked and offers to come to me straight away. I tell her no, I just need to sort myself out. I see Jake's brother outside a door adjacent to ICU. He's been on the phone. I just go to him and we cry together.

People start to leave and it's just me, Jake's brother and his wife. A nurse comes in and gives me a clear plastic bag with Jake's belongings. It's just so incredibly sad.

All the staff are very quiet and respectful especially given this is a huge and busy hospital.

I can't comprehend that he's gone.

Bob, his wife and I walk out of the hospital towards the car park where they are parked.

I suddenly realise I don't have the overnight bag Jake came in with. It has his phone in it so we walk back and tell the nurse.

She finally locates it after about forty-five minutes. It is now gone 3 a.m. and we're walking once again to the car.

I notice there is a full moon and Bob's wife points this out as well and I say, 'Perhaps Jake will come back as a wolf.' Normal.

I also ask them if I need to change my surname. The things you think of…

They ask if I want to go home with them but I don't want to. I just want to be back at our home, so they drive me there.

After they leave, I realise I am alone. My husband has died.

My perfect Jake of twenty-four years has gone.

I'm in a bubble. A bubble filled with shit.

I just cry and cry and cry.

✳✳✳

The Next Day

I have not slept and I am still in the front room wearing one of Jake's jumpers and a pair of his socks.

I eat crisps and drink coffee.

I look at my Facebook page and change my profile picture to one of Jake and I. I forgot that when you change your profile picture it notifies the world and his wife.

My mobile goes nuts. I suppose I better say something 'official' as people are genuinely concerned.

On Facebook, I post:

Dear friends,

My world and partner in 'wine' left this world yesterday due to complications following an operation. No words can explain the effect this has had on me, but I one hundred percent know he'd be telling me to buck the fuck up.

Some of you that are already aware have said some beautiful words and I genuinely appreciate them. I absolutely never ever thought I'd be doing this, and myself and the rest of our family are devastated but together we will get through this.

I'm just so glad we did so many amazing things together. He will always be my husband and my life. I love you, Jake, forever 🖤

Simone

I get sixty-nine comments and that makes me smile.

My best mate calls me. She asks if I want her to come over and I tell her no. I don't want to see anyone.

She says tough tits and informs me she's en route. She turns up with a packet of fags (she says she thought these were more useful than flowers) and a huge cuddle and just smokes and talks with me. I am inconsolable.

Flowers turn up from someone, I can't remember who.

Charley answers the door and brings them in to me. She stays for a few hours and I think I'm delirious.

There is this enormous lump. It's sitting kind of halfway between my chest and my stomach. It won't go. I've not even had a shower. I don't know how to think. It doesn't seem real.

Mum and Dad are on their way and Greg and his wife Natalie.

I talk to them about what happened and manage to do so without completely breaking down. I love all these people but I really just want to be on my own. I want to just sit and cry and cry.

I can hear Mum and Dad and Greg and Natalie talking about me whilst I'm making tea and coffee, something about me being strong.

Once they all leave, I go into the kitchen under the guise of eating something that is not beige. I see Jake's box of cornflakes and the water bottle that was in his overnight bag that he got from the vending machine at the hotel. He used it to take some tablets the night before the op. This makes me so sad. I just sit on the floor and cry. I'm not even sure I even want to be here anymore. I don't want a life without Jake. I love our life.

It takes all my strength to make the call to the bereavement line at the hospital today.

They are very nice and offer their condolences but, in my head, I really do wonder why they ask you to call within twenty-four hours. It does not make any sense to me, but it's 'protocol' and we go through the motions. The woman on the other end of the phone prepares me for the fact that she needs to ask a few delicate questions and asks me if I know whether or not Jake will be buried or cremated.

I think, *Seriously, love, you can fuck right off. I can barely wipe my own arse at the moment.*

I get that they need to know, but really, twenty-four hours after the event? This isn't a dear old nan popping her clogs at ninety-three, this is my husband. Together for twenty-four years and married for eleven. He wasn't supposed to die. The operation was supposed to make him better.

I answer her questions as best I can and she tells me I will hear from the coroner shortly but does say, because it's just before Christmas, there might be a delay.

Apparently dying before Christmas is like posting a Christmas card on Christmas Eve. I've not even thought about Christmas.

My sister Polly comes over this evening. She just listens to me but I am a complete mess. I know I need people around me but I keep pushing them away. I know I do.

For some reason, I am watching endless episodes of *MasterChef*. I cannot bear to watch anything Jake and I watched together. He hated that Greg bloke, called him Pig Boy.

I talk to Polly about my engagement ring. I am

obsessed about selling it and ask my sister to look online about roughly how much I would get. I rationalise this by explaining the ring was a bit of a bugbear between Jake. It was bloody expensive and I tell her it means nothing to me. She tells me not to be too hasty.

Thank God I listened to her.

Note to anyone going through any form of grief: do not knee jerk on any decision. I was a hundred percent still in complete shock. In fact, in hindsight, I would recommend you do not make any decisions bigger than what to have for dinner for the first two or three months.

I do chuck away his medication though; I don't associate that with Jake.

I am also becoming obsessed with the local news. A man with a young family has gone missing after a night out. It's not too far away and the police are obviously concerned about him. His wife is on the TV making an appeal to anyone who may have seen him the night he disappeared. I don't know why but it is really affecting me. Maybe it's because I can see and feel her pain?

I keep thinking, *At least I know where Jake is.* I cannot imagine not knowing and constantly wondering where they are. I think it could be worse but I'm not thinking straight.

It's just gone 11 p.m. and my doorbell goes. I panic straight away. I don't know why as the worst has already happened but it must be instinct.

I open the door tentatively and it's a policeman. I must look stricken as he tells me, 'Don't worry,' and goes on to say a fence at number 45 is down and they think it could've been an attempted break-in and have I noticed anything.

I almost laugh. Seriously? I explain my circumstances and the young copper looks mortified, apologises and ticks me off his list.

I go to bed on the sofa again in Jake's clothes.

***

Go to Mum and Dad's today with Polly, Dave and their daughter Nicole. We don't stay for too long.

I'm staying at Polly's tonight. I'm not sure how I feel about it. People keep saying I shouldn't be on my own so I want to see how it goes.

I feel so angsty. Polly and Dave try so hard to look after me, frantically turning off any Christmas music from the radio and telly. It just makes me laugh to see the sheer panic on their faces.

We get pizza and Dave pops out to see a mate for a couple of hours. I share a margherita pizza with Nicole and we try to watch some shit on telly. Polly's sitting so close to me. She's like a little limpet. I just don't want to cry even though Polly tells me it's okay.

We go to bed and I do sleep.

I wake up with Polly next to me and it is all I can do not to crumble.

I just want to be at home. I feel closer to Jake there. I miss all of his things.

We go into town to get a couple of bits. I buy some Christmas cards and presents for two of Jake's kids, who are thirty and forty respectively, before Christmas.

Polly is watching me like a hawk. I know I look a mess. I haven't showered and I am acutely aware I probably look like a crack addict. But it's okay. Polly's on the watch for any fuckers who might dare to try to interact with me.

Once I'm home, I keep cleaning.

Jake was in charge of the housework. I just worked to keep him in the lifestyle he'd become accustomed to. Tidy house, tidy mind. TBH, my mind's fucked.

I go to take some rubbish out to the bins at the bottom of my garden. It's dark so I can't see fuck all. I notice there's light coming from inside the bin liner. I grab for it and it's a little spotlight, one of those ones you can get from Poundland. Jake used them for the garden sometimes. I use it to see the bottom of the garden. I think, *Maybe Jake put that there so I didn't fall arse over tit when taking the rubbish out.* He was thoughtful like that.

Maybe it's a sign.

Polly keeps checking if I'm eating, although, to be honest, I'm about three stone overweight so I could live off my reserves for a fair while. This is a result of Jake not only being a feeder but a fucking fantastic cook.

I let Polly know I'm having a balanced meal this evening

with a toasted cheese sandwich and a packet of Frazzles and some chocolate milk. #iamclearly12

I've also progressed from *MasterChef* to serial killer documentaries.

I find a note from Jake in my purse. He wrote it a couple of years ago. It says: 'You make me happier than wine.' High praise indeed.

Jake's siblings make a WhatsApp group for us all and consists of Jake's brother, Jake's five sisters and me. This is a first to have us all together. Being a big family, there can sometimes be a bit of friction, so I suppose something good needs to come of what has happened.

I go to bed in the marital bed tonight. I'm utterly exhausted. I put Jake's dressing gown on his side of the bed so it feels like he's next to me. Just as I'm dropping off, I feel something grab me round the waist. It makes me jump but I settle as I think it's Jake.

✳✳✳

The next morning, I realise I need to get some shopping, I can't handle the thought of walking into town and as Jake did all of the shopping, I can't access his Ocado account, so I register myself and do my first online food shop.

I am quite chuffed I managed to organise this.

I send my completed shopping list to Polly. It consists of mainly Pringles. I haven't yet felt the need to drink alcohol. I think I realise that drinking would send me even lower so I settle for sugar free Vimto instead.

I go into the kitchen, look out the stable door and there are eleven magpies on a roof a few houses away. I start manically Googling if this means something. Always looking for a sign. There's fuck all on Google but I'm taking that one. It must mean something.

Jake's brother Bob and his wife Sam come over. It is quite nice as Bob is talking about Jake. I love hearing people talk about him.

Polly comes over late afternoon and we sit, chat and smoke fags. She doesn't smoke.

***

Two of Jake's sisters, Patricia and Alice, come over today. Alice and Jake didn't really talk for numerous reasons but I let her back into our lives. At this moment, it feels like the right thing.

She is okay but when she starts telling me how her new boyfriend leaves her little Post-it notes with romantic quotes, I want to throat punch her. Fuck off.

Patricia tells me my house looks like a show house. Jake would be proud.

Patricia calls me in the evening to say she's heard a song on the radio. It reminded her of Jake and she cried. She says this is the first time she has cried. It's heart breaking. My heart is in pieces for me and for them.

Dinner is a mini pizza and some Wotsits. I add some olives for my veg allowance.

I venture into town to meet two of Jake's sisters.

Just walking into town makes me cry. It's just horrendous. So many memories and it hurts seeing all these other fuckers getting on with their lives, looking all Christmassy and shit.

I keep my head down willing myself not to see any landmarks that remind me of us or, heaven forbid, bump into people we might know.

This lump between my throat and stomach just won't go. It's restricting my breathing; just a permanent reminder of the loss.

We meet for brunch in Bill's. I chose this place as me and Jake had never been there together. It's okay in Bill's but I crumble when they ask me how I'm doing. I do manage avocado on toast and a black coffee.

Patricia calls me this evening again and the sisters want to arrange a meet up for all of the family round her place on the Saturday before Christmas. I'm not sure if I can handle so many people but Polly said she'd come so I think I'll say yes.

✳✳✳

I speak to my boss and tell her I'd like to come into work, not to work but just to talk to them and work out what to do.

I know I am lucky as they've been good. The HR manager says the two or three days' compassionate leave stance is a joke and tells me I can take as long as I need.

I tell them I would like to come back to the office between Christmas and New Year. I think it'll be quieter with not so many people to have to deal with.

When I'm talking to them about Jake and what happened, I have to physically squeeze my cheeks with my thumb and forefinger squishing them together to stop me crying.

I see a couple of colleagues but I am in bits as I leave. I walk into town on the way back to get fags. I appear to be a smoker. Bollocks.

I also buy some ice cream from Waitrose that cost almost the same as my fags. Jake would murder me.

I am, however, progressing on the food front. Upon unpacking my food delivery, I see Jake made me a few meals that I forgot about that he popped in the freezer. He made them before the op as he knew I'd be home alone whilst he should have been recovering.

Didn't quite turn out like that.

***

Got Trixie and Scott coming over today. I think she might

try to persuade me to go out to the pub. She brings me a 'rescue box' with perfume and chocolate and a homemade pebble shaped like a heart and painted red. She is so kind.

I relay the events to them both. It's so hard. I have to squeeze my cheeks together again to stop me from crying. Trixie says we should have a pub lunch. Scott scarpers and walks into town. Don't blame him at all. We have fish and chips in The Stoke and I feel okayish. I have a glass of wine and another. Actually, I have a bottle. Trixie sticks to mini bottles of Prosecco.

Once Trixie and Scott depart, it really hits me. I blame the booze as well. I wish I could get rid of this feeling of complete and utter loss of control. I just can't see a future without him.

I book myself a tattoo. Jake hates tattoos but I want to get one done in honour of him. This is definitely a knee jerk reaction. I think I'm going round the twist but I've done it now. Booked for 10th January 2020.

I have also ordered £100 plus of skincare. I don't know if it's because I look like shit or whether I'm trying to distract myself with presents for me that I really can't afford, but there's no one to judge me so fuck it.

***

Polly's husband gives us a lift to Jake's sister's for our Christmas get together. We decide it's a good idea to sip some 'tinnies' on our journey for some Dutch courage. Two tinnies each over a twenty-minute car ride. Awesome.

We park outside and my guts are churning. Polly must be shitting it too as she's never even met these people.

I can see people through the kitchen window. It looks rammed.

We walk in and everyone is really lovely. It's nice to see Jake's two daughters.

Introductions are made and I position myself in the conservatory and keep getting my glass filled up with red.

Polly's so good; proper socialising with my other family.

There is so much food. Polly sticks pieces of random hors d'oeuvres in my gob. I don't think they're going to cut the mustard in soaking up the amount of red wine I've consumed thus far.

I give one of Jake's nieces a massive container of Black Jacks. He bought them for her a couple of weeks before the operation. He did it as he remembers being at a christening or some kind of communion and he was feeding her the sweets to turn her tongue black so when she took the 'body of Christ' wafer she'd look like something out of *The Exorcist*. He loved to wind people up. She told me she'd never ever open them and her kids were banned from eating them.

The estranged sister makes a big scene about something

and sods off crying. I tell the other sisters I really don't give a shit. Today is about Jake, not about her.

Jake's cousin tells me about her daughter who lost her husband too. She tells me how I will be okay and that her daughter has found somebody new. I want to throat punch her.

I know I tell both of Jake's daughters how proud he was of them. He genuinely was. He just wasn't that great at expressing it.

I am sitting on the floor, totally plastered. I don't know how I manage it but I fall backwards from a sitting position. Wine spills on the carpet. Bugger. Think it's time I left.

Me and Polly stagger indoors, open some more wine and eat some crisps.

✳✳✳

I get told about my hilarities from last night in detail from all of Jake's family. They seem to think I was not offensive.

However, we've now got 'champagne gate' and Patricia is raging that somebody has apparently stolen a bottle of the stuff from her wine rack last night and she's not impressed.

I quickly check my bag just in case I pilfered it. I didn't. Plus, I don't really like champagne. I mean, I'll drink it if I'm forced, but it's not a drink of choice.

I speak to the coroners today. They still need to establish the cause of death. So, I will not be able to make any plans until that's done. The coroner's assistant is pleasant enough and tells me he'll keep me updated throughout.

If I'm honest, I'm in no hurry to have the funeral. I really don't want to say goodbye to him.

***

My work have been brilliant. They're paying for grief counselling for me and I've got my first appointment today: Christmas Eve. Polly's coming with me. My little protector.

Even travelling to the train station is an effort. When you lose someone, you feel so vulnerable. It's like you were part of a couple and as that's shattered, you feel only half of yourself and open for people to attack you. It's a really awful feeling. I can barely speak to people or make eye contact.

Polly won't let anything bad happen to me.

I shuffle to the inside two seats nearest to the train door and Polly sits next to me. I need to sit there as I feel protected from others.

The counsellor's office is about ten minutes away from the train station in a little village not far from where I live. The walk there is pleasant and Polly is trying to keep my mind on just getting there!

During the walk to the actual premises, I go to walk over three drain covers. Apparently, it's unlucky and Polly drags me away. I tell her I have been fairly unlucky so far. I'm not convinced it will make much of a difference to my life now.

We are so ridiculously early that we have to take a

walk to pretty much the other side of the village just to waste time. I have never been one for tardiness but this is ridiculous. I am about forty-five minutes too early. I cannot even smoke as I would rather not have my first session stinking of cigarettes.

It is early too, before 9 a.m., so fuck all is open. After some wandering around, we make the move to the office with still ten minutes to go.

I check in and take a seat with Polly next to me. The building is quaint, all low ceilings and beams. Tranquil lift music is playing softly and there is a heap of magazines to browse through. There are also Cadbury Eclairs in a bowl. We take one each and pocket them for the walk back to the station.

A patient comes out of one of the rooms; I am trying to guess why they are there. Are they grief stricken, depressed, anxious or all of the above? They look normal. Do I look normal?

My counsellor is lovely. She listens and she does make me feel somewhat normal… ish. She tells me this process is a long and tough road and I just need to go with what I am feeling.

I tell her I don't want to carry on. I say I want to go and be with Jake. She asks me what Jake would think of that. I say he'd want to be with me. She asks what happens if I do end it and then don't get reunited with him. That makes me think. Part of me wants to believe that if I did end it all, I would be reunited with Jake but she's saying maybe it's not like that. Maybe we have to do our time. Maybe he would not want me to end it.

I like her and feel a little bit more positive afterwards.

On the train journey home, as we get to our destination, I feel for my train ticket but cannot find it anywhere. I am frantically going through my pockets and my handbag. Nothing. I start to panic.

Polly takes charge and says she will sort it. We walk to the barriers in the station to get out and she has a quick word with the guard and we walk straight through.

I do not hear what she says but I'm sure it goes something like, 'I am a carer for my special sister. She will have a complete meltdown if you shout at her. So, please don't.'

I am grateful for her intervention.

I seem to go from one to three thousand in ten seconds. I used to be fairly consistent.

I am home now.

Polly gets picked up by Dave. I open the two Christmas presents Jake had wrapped up for me before the operation. He left them in our airing cupboard in an effort to conceal them.

One present is a pair of PJs from M&S. They are very cute with a cat print and a matching cat sleep mask. The receipt is still in with the present. It says, 'In case you want to exchange them.' That will never happen.

The second present is a beautiful cream bobble hat with a little fur bobble and a gold stamp on the rim of the hat. That makes me smile. I had been asking Jake to buy me a bobble hat from Primark that had two bobbles that looked like bear ears. He refused and said I was a forty-seven-year-old woman. This was obviously a compromise.

I go to bed in my new PJs and my bobble hat.

Christmas Day

I have literally not stopped crying this morning. It's unbearable. I cannot get my shit together. Jake made Christmas so special for me as he knew I loved it.

For a couple of years, Jake made me his own advent calendar for Christmas. A present every day until Christmas. Anything from a novelty mug or chocolates to perfume and shoes. My male work colleagues hated him as he put them to shame.

I am supposed to be staying over at Polly's today but I just don't think I can be away from home. Being here makes me feel close to Jake and I don't want him to be alone on Christmas Day. Polly tells me to do whatever feels right.

Mum and Dad pick me up en route to Polly's. I want to be strong for them and my niece as she's only twelve.

Mum and Dad ask how I am.

'I'm fine,' I say.

Once we get to Polly's, it seems to be a joint decision that the best thing to do is start on the sherry consumption. Me, Polly and Mum all get stuck in.

Mother does not usually drink, so after a couple of sherrys, she is well on her way. She starts telling me she can see Jake by Polly's back door. What the fuck is he doing at Polly's?

I can see Dave is trying to distract her as she is now having a full-on conversation with Jake by the back door.

Sherry finished, wine opened. Dave, my brother-in-law, makes Mum a large G and T.

Poor old Dad is just watching us all get drunk. Poor bugger is the designated driver.

Okay, so this has escalated. Dave made Christmas dinner, but we're standing around the kitchen table dunking roast potatoes into a jug of gravy. Dad is sitting on the sofa with Mum who has a bowl under her chin and she is throwing up. He is mopping her chin and laughing.

An hour or so later, I decide I want to go home and Polly says she will come with me. We leave with Mum who is practically passed out in the passenger seat. Polly and me are in the back seat and there's a bottle of half opened Prosecco wedged between us. We obviously insisted that we take it with us as we clearly need it.

Dad starts the car and then, all of a sudden, there is this

huge whoosh. The cork from the Prosecco has shot out, narrowly misses Dad's head and hits the windscreen with Prosecco splashing everywhere. Mum mumbles it was Jake trying to kill her.

Me and Polly are back at mine now. It can't be much fun for her. She's left her husband and my niece at home and is try to console me. Much booze is consumed.

✳✳✳

Boxing Day

I feel fabulous.

Polly is in my bed next to me sleeping on my side of the bed. It is strange how I am on Jake's side.

We make some toast and Dave comes and picks Polly up about lunchtime. I spend the rest of the day sleeping and trying to forget. Not much different from any other Boxing Day.

✳✳✳

First day back to work. The hardest part is walking to the office. There's hardly anyone in. One of the ladies from another department comes and kneels by me and tells me how sorry she is. This makes me cry.

The walk home after work is the worst. Jake used to

meet me at the top of the road opposite my office regularly. Everything reminds me of Jake.

I can picture him so clearly standing at the top of the road by the road name, leaning casually in his new puffer jacket that I bought him to go to NYC this year.

I literally can't see anything as I'm crying so hard. If anyone clocks me, they'll definitely think I'm deranged.

The tiredness that comes after this is all-consuming and I can't get rid of this knot in my guts.

I message David, Jake's son. It was his thirtieth a little while ago and I have bought him a present. He didn't come to the get together pre-Christmas.

He says he will come and pick it up but says he doesn't want to come in as he's not ready.

He pops over and collects said present. We hug and don't say much.

I am watching some shit eighties film set in NYC and it makes me think of our trip to NYC earlier this year for Jake's birthday.

It has been over two weeks since Jake went away and it's not getting any easier. In fact, it's getting more real and that's bloody scary.

One of the real trigger issues for me is planning. Even people speaking about New Year's resolutions winds me up. I cannot think about my future. I can't because I don't want a future without Jake.

I have just finished a bottle of Chianti that was on our

'favourites' list on Ocado. I thought I would buy it for Jake. I crapped myself when the delivery turned up as I couldn't find the bottle.

Turns out it was only a half a bottle which is why I couldn't find it initially. That will also be why it was only £6.99. I have no idea why it appeared as a favourite as: a) we'd never purposefully buy a half bottle of wine, and b) my online account isn't linked to Jake's. Maybe they go by the address.

I cry all the time. I miss him so much.

I tried to recreate one of Jake's dishes today. I think he would have been proud of me as it tasted pretty similar.

I vow I am going to spend the rest of life making my husband proud of me.

Jake's siblings have been incredible but my sister has been my rock. If she was not around, I'm pretty sure I would have tried to top myself.

People tell me to concentrate on all the wonderful things we did together. This, in theory, completely makes sense. The problem is, when I do reminisce, I am just completely overwhelmed with sadness that I will never do anything with him again.

I am surprised at the perception of us as a couple. We really were quite highly thought of. I thought most people thought we were a pair of cunts.

I still think Jake's going to walk thought the door with a load of shopping and I see him everywhere. Walking down our road, when I walk to work, in town. Everywhere.

Then, when I get closer, I realise it isn't him, even though I know it couldn't be. Then I cry a little bit more. It just isn't fair.

I hope he is up there kicking it up with his best friends and Mum and Dad.

I am genuinely devastated for Jake as well and not just for me. He wanted to live. I know he loved our life together.

✳✳✳

I went to work again today. I feel like the new girl that nobody wants to run into in the toilets. I can't blame them. I'd avoid me too.

One of the girls in the office asks me how my Christmas was. She asks if I just had a chilled one. Instead of saying it was fucking awful and I spent two days with the biggest knot in my stomach and a feeling of utter despair that just doesn't go, I say, 'It was fine,' then walk to the loos and slump down in one of the cubicles sobbing.

Maybe some people just do not think about others. Maybe I was selfish too?

I am dreading tomorrow. I don't want to start a year without Jake. I am not convinced I can do this. He was my future.

Why did he die and why did he leave me?

Deep down, I know there is no way he would have

wanted to leave me; I know he would've fought. He would know how scared I would be right now.

I am honestly not sure if I can keep it together.

One minute, I am cleaning then I'm cooking feeling okayish and the next minute, I'm back to being a complete wreck. The emptiness is unbearable. That is the worse feeling: utter emptiness.

Our memories make me cry because that is what they are. Memories. I want to imagine our future.

The pain I feel knowing I will never do anything else with Jake is hideous. It makes me wish I had cherished him a little bit more and let him know how much I love him.

The day of the operation replays in my head like an annoying song playing repeatedly.

Maybe I didn't check on him early enough. Why was I worried that the hospital would think I was being neurotic? I had a right to be neurotic. I think I knew something was wrong all along.

I remember Jake's consultant told me that he would be in hospital for at least eight weeks because of the dialysis. Do you know what my first thought was when he said that? I thought, *Christ, that's going to be a shitter over Christmas.*

I would be so fucking grateful if I could visit Jake now.

However, I can't and he is gone.

NYE

I am only working until 12 p.m. today.

Polly came over this afternoon for a couple of hours. My neighbour knocked on my door and poor Polly had to answer it. The nosy mare wanted to know what was going on. Polly got rid of her.

I have slacked off all invites to do anything this evening. I just want to have a glass of wine and talk to Jake… in my head.

I open a nice bottle of Fleurie.

His oldest daughter messages me and it seems she is not in a great place either. She lives by the coast and tells me she is walking to the shops to get a bottle of red and asks for my recommendations.

I tell her to try a bottle of Fleurie. It's very nice. She finds a bottle and says she is going to walk along the beach and have a glass. Not in a vagrant wino way but just looking out at the sea.

I know how much this is all hurting his family and it devastates me.

I make it to midnight and only half a bottle of wine. I am not great drinking on my own so I try to keep it to a minimum.

January 2020

My husband died last year.

For some reason, just acknowledging this really hurts. It's as if I'm letting him go and I feel like I have been hit by a truck.

Yesterday was the hardest day.

I don't believe he's not coming home. My heart literally aches on a continual basis. I am struggling to understand how this has actually happened. My head is in a constant mess and I feel like I am going crazy. I miss him so much and feel completely lost without him. Nothing anyone says can bring him back and I am just so very sad.

In the back of my mind, I know I'm also going to have to deal with the formalities very soon and that's filling me with utter dread. I really want to be okay but I just feel so overwhelmed.

One of the spotlights underneath our kitchen cabinets keeps on flashing. I have convinced myself that this surely must be another 'sign'.

I'm trying to forward think and make decisions and try to be a grown-up. I am filled with dread and fear as I'm scared I am going to fuck it up. I was not the responsible adult in our relationship. I am not ready to adult yet.

The family WhatsApp group is filling up with fucking sad songs. I don't open these ones. I can't listen to the songs; my heart is already broken. Why are they doing this? How can they listen to all of these songs?

I have booked a doctor's appointment. I've never been to this surgery before. The doctor I see is male. He is incredibly kind and when I ask for something to help me get through this, he says how I'm feeling is completely normal and the fact that I'm having counselling will help. He tells me everything I am doing is good and rather than prescribe me medication just yet, he asks me to come and see him again in a week or two.

I just want something to numb the pain. The flashbacks I keep getting when I close my eyes are horrific. I picture the resuscitation and all the people surrounding Jake and the noise but the strange silence all at the same time. Sometimes this can drag me into such a dark place, it is difficult to want to be alive.

Bob and Sam are coming over and we are meeting in the pub. Trixie is also coming over and staying the night.

The pub is nice. Bob keeps talking about Jake which I love. They ask me to tell them about how Jake and I met. We also talk about mine and Jake's sex life. Poor old Bob does not really need to know about his brother's massive penis but Sam and Trixie are laughing their arses off.

I finally buck up the courage to go and get a round at the bar. I honestly haven't dipped my hand in my pocket since what happened 'happened'. I stand at the bar. It's not too busy but my head feels like it's swimming and I'm stuttering when ordering. My confidence is at rock bottom but I make it back with a bottle of wine, a bottle of Prosecco and a pint of cider. Not too shabby for four of us.

Bob and Sam leave early evening and me and Trixie carry on for a bit. We keep saying we'll have one for the road. Pretty certain we went home via Penzance.

We get back to mine half cut and blow up Trixie's airbed and she takes a delightful photo of me falling arse over tit in the front room.

We make a pact that we will do this once a month.

✳✳✳

Trixie left before lunch and I am lounging on the settee eating toast, breadsticks and Smarties.

I do not really feel anything today. I am just numb.

This is the problem with drinking. Whilst I am with company, I feel okay but as soon as I am on my own and the hangover kicks in, I feel dreadful.

There is so much going on in my head and I'm struggling to decipher what needs doing or sorting out first.

I am looking though my emails and know I should really see if I can chase up the airline to make sure our upcoming holiday is cancelled. We were due to go to Portugal in June.

Why is there a special bereavement telephone number for the airline? It seems crazy. I do not want to speak to anyone. I suppose some people have others that will make these calls and I know that either my family or Jake's would help out but part of me needs to take some control.

I make the call and they are okay. I have to do the usual and send them evidence of Jake's death. It does make me wonder who would make something up like this, but I guess there are some sickos about.

They say they will come back to me ASAP.

I decide I am going to start writing about how Jake and I met. I just don't want to ever not remember. I also think it may be a positive thing for me. I might write in this diary. We will see how I feel.

Okay, so I am into this. Here it goes.

We met in 1996. I was the manager of some shit costume jewellery shop aimed at teenyboppers. Jake was the manager of an Italian designer wear shop that was opposite my shop. I remember seeing him looking over at me over a gondola (a display unit, not a Venetian boat) from his shop.

I was in a relationship with my partner of six years and fully mortgaged up. We were not happy though. I had settled down too early at seventeen.

I wasn't really attracted to Jake at the time. He was persistent though and he kept inviting me over for fresh coffee before we opened our respective shops in the morning.

I was a bit scared of him actually. He was a grown-up but I was only twenty-four.

One morning, we were having coffee as normal. He kicked the main door to the shop closed, pushed me up against the wall and kissed me. Properly.

That was it. Complete and utter lust.

Jake didn't tell me he was married for a while. If I'm honest, I think I kind of knew, but I ignored it. I was young and in an unhappy relationship and Jake made me feel like a real woman.

It wasn't long at all before I was totally and completely in love with him. I knew it was reciprocated when we were in a taxi to where I lived with my ex. The taxi pulled up at the end of the road to covertly drop me off and as I was shutting the door, he said, 'I love you.'

I went back and said, 'What?'

He said, 'Nothing.'

Then as I shut the door, he said I love you again and drove off.

That was the start of our twenty-four years together.

***

An old friend visits me this evening. Although it's nice to see her, we've grown apart over the last couple of years. Just lives going in different directions.

I explain what happened the day Jake, you know, and

she cries silently with me.

I tell her how the coroners are dicking around and still don't know the cause and that everything is delayed because of Christmas.

She tells me how she saw her aunt after she died and that it was awful and she doesn't recommend me seeing Jake. I know she means well but now I can't stop thinking about how she described her dead aunt's face. I remember Jake as asleep, not dead.

This morning I change our bed clothes.

Note to anyone that loses a loved one: wait a little, don't rush. I regret not lying in Jake's festering side of the bed.

I found a quote today: 'My journey has not yet ended. I have a road to follow, but I know I will reunite with my perfect man at the end.' I love this.

Greg and Natalie come over this evening. They keep telling me how brave I am. I don't feel it one little bit. I make endless cups of tea and coffee, anything to be out of the room and alone with my thoughts. Greg tells me how he thought Jake looked ill the day he drove us both to the hospital. That cuts through me.

***

Tattoo Day

I'm not at all nervous. Polly comes with me, obviously.

The tattoo artist has drawn me a mock-up of the tattoo I requested, but it's not what I asked for. I panic as my email was quite specific.

I tell him that is not what I emailed. He shows me my email. He's right, that is what I asked for. I must have asked for the more elaborate design in my own fucking head.

I can feel myself going red and my cheeks are heating up as I'm embarrassed. I apologise and explain my circumstances and he tells me to hold on and he then redraws it. It takes about twenty-five minutes and he's done it perfectly.

It doesn't hurt at all and only takes twenty minutes or so. He's a really nice guy and doesn't even charge me extra for the 'bespoke and emergency' design!

I am meeting two of Jake's sisters at an Italian restaurant in town. Polly is coming as well.

We walk into town and it takes me ages to remember where the restaurant is even though I've been there a few times. Polly's got Google Maps out as I am incapable and she heads in the other direction. Transpires we've walked past the bloody place twice. Once we go into the restaurant, I freeze.

It is heaving and I feel like I'm about to have a panic attack. Polly seamlessly takes over and checks us both in.

She's becoming the big sister.

Jake's sisters turn up. I show them the tattoo. I'm not convinced they are that impressed but I love it.

I was perusing the menu last night and had picked out a nice bottle of red wine for us to toast Jake with, but in the end Patricia chooses as she wasn't keen on my choice. Ridiculously, I go along with it.

We have a nice time, stay for a couple of hours and make the usual innuendos when the waiter turns up with a giant pepper mill.

I'm okay when I'm with company and loosened by wine. I suppose I just put on the mask and brazen it out. 'I'm fine,' I say.

Patricia almost falls down the stairs coming out of the place. It's a rickety old building so that's an excuse but mainly because she is tipsy. We congregate outside and wait for her. For some reason, she goes back up the stairs to steal a napkin and shoves it down her tights. She whips it out once she's outside and Liz says she thinks it's because she might wet herself.

This is my life now.

I get home. Polly goes home. The wine buzz is wearing off and I am alone.

I can't stop thinking of how sad it is that Jake had to go. I wish it was me. I truly would give absolutely anything to have Jake back. I feel sorry that he's not here. He had FOMO and lived life to the full.

People have been so kind but it doesn't distract from the fact he's been taken away from me. Life is not fair. My world and best friend isn't here anymore and that makes me so, so sad.

I don't know how to handle this. Jake would know what to do. I don't.

I am eating chocolate in the vain attempt that it takes away some of the pain. It doesn't.

The pain is off the Richter scale. I feel utterly helpless, out of control and without any purpose.

I say out loud, 'Please come back to me, Jake.'

✳✳✳

I actually thought about ending it last night. Did you know if you look online about suicide, rather than giving you helpful tips on how to end it, like how many tablets you have to take to go to sleep forever, it gives you the telephone number for The Samaritans which, for your records, is 116 123. It took every fibre of my body not to either:

- Reach for the pills and vodka
- Dial the number

Today, I feel slightly better. I do, however, have this irrational fear that Jake is cold wherever he is. I feel I want to cover him up and make him cosy.

I am trying to be practical.

I look online about all the things you have to do when somebody dies. They say as follows:

- Obtain a medical certificate for the cause of death
- Register the death and for that, you require the above
- Choose a funeral director
- Let people know about the death

The coroners call me, finally. They explain to me that there has to be a post-mortem on 17th January as they cannot establish the cause of Jake's death.

They at least tell me he is at our local hospital. I have been having nightmares about where he is. Is he cold, alone? At least now I know he is close to me; the hospital is about two miles from me

The coroners tell me there is nothing sinister going on despite their lack of communication with me. They advise me that the hospital is at full capacity and they are running approximately three weeks behind. Behind what? Fuck off.

I make an enquiry for an 'all inclusive' funeral package and click the online enquiry form. Although I am no nearer to having a date for the funeral, people are starting to ask. It does not seem over a month since he went.

I am told by a friend that I can apply for a 'bereavement payment'. It is a lump sum of approximately £3k and then monthly payments of approximately £100 for eighteen months. The lump sum is to help with the cost of the funeral.

Jake had no pension or savings so this is something to help me. I have no intention at all of asking for help from his family or mine. I want to do this myself. It's again all about being able to control something.

I start looking through the contacts on Jake's mobile as I need to get hold of people for when the funeral does happen, but I don't make good progress as I get distracted by reading all the text messages he has sent me over the years.

I have spoken to the funeral directors. They're really very good. We decide on a date of 7th February 2020 which we think gives the coroners plenty of time to finish any investigations.

The funeral director assures me they will handle everything and all I need to do is stump up the cash. I go for a low-key, no-frills cremation with a non-religious service for about sixty people.

They put me in touch with the celebrant/humanist and he's coming over next week to talk through the details.

Jake's youngest daughter is coming over this evening. I crave seeing his family. It makes me feel closer to Jake, but I am fully aware she didn't have an ideal relationship with her dad since he left their mother (his first wife). Although he became close with his eldest, not so much with his youngest daughter. He has a son from his second marriage and is close to him.

His youngest daughter has written some beautiful stuff on Instagram about me but she seems detached from Jake.

We do talk about him and she says she is sorry, but she goes on to tell me about all the shit things she remembers from her childhood with him.

Jake left the girls when they were young, only saw them at the weekends and had other priorities at the time. He knew this was shit. Jake knew he'd made mistakes with the kids. He was the first to admit it and tried to rebuild the relationships in his own way.

She tells me how, because he left, the girls and their mum moved into this ramshackle place with rats and everything, and how it traumatised her. She says she only remembers him taking her and her sister to pubs and feeding them crisps and coke and that he didn't act like their father.

She leaves after a few hours and I honestly feel utterly drained. I know there is love in there… somewhere.

What I am most upset about is that I didn't stop what she was saying about him. I told her he was the adult in the relationship and it was down to him to make the effort. I said all of this in Jake's home and it made me feel quite sick with anxiety but also guilt.

I feel like I have betrayed him but I want the kids to be okay.

Our mutual friend Cora has arranged for us to go to mine and Jake's local pub this evening to discuss requirements for the 'after party'.

I have been avoiding this place since Jake went. We did go to this particular pub frequently. It's a pretty pub with open fires and twinkly lights and is clean and the food is good.

Walking in there is dreadful but Polly is with me. It is a mixture of the familiarity of the pub mixed with the weirdness of not having Jake by my side.

Cora takes over which is fine. I want her to.

The manager of the pub comes over and introduces herself. She seems okay but I have never seen her before. She shows me the buffet menus they can offer for the 'after party'.

I am drawn to one option that has foods on it that I know Jake would like. Spicy shit. I say I'd like to go for that. Cora intervenes and suggests the cheaper option. I know she's just trying to save me money but frankly I don't give a shit. Jake's worth it. Polly says I should make the choice right for me.

I choose the wine I'd like served and order twelve bottles of Prosecco and twelve bottles of red for everyone to have a drink when they get to the *after party*.

I am not calling it a wake. Ever.

We also go for some soft drinks (not many, due to calibre of attendees) and beer and ale.

They all keep buying me wine. I'm okay with this.

He was really loved you know, Jake was.

Cora asks more about the funeral arrangements asking if it will be a religious ceremony. I advise not. Jake was a Catholic but definitely a lapsed Catholic.

The manager of the pub says she will finalise the figures for me and send them across. I ask her to send them to Cora so she can make sure all is okay. It's just something I really don't need to take charge of.

Suppose that's another job done.

✳✳✳

I ordered loads of shabby chic photo frames the other day. I put them up this afternoon. I had no hammer so used a red glass paperweight I've got. It worked. You've got to think outside the box sometimes.

The front room has turned into a shrine for Jake.

I wish I could cup his face right now and kiss it. I am just so grateful that I had twenty-four years with this man.

The coroners contact me today and tell me there has to be a histology examination. I'm told they will need to remove some of Jake's organs in order to run pathology and histology tests on them. They tell me they have to take his heart, his spinal cord and parts of his kidneys and lungs. This makes me feel sick. The thought of them removing Jake's heart feels so wrong and I keep worrying that Jake is cold and alone on a slab.

I hate what they are doing to him. I can't sleep.

***

Today, I let the coroners know the date of the funeral so they are aware of the deadlines.

My contact there asks me if I want Jake's organs repatriated. I don't want to think about parts of him being discarded or thrown away or stuffed into his body.

I tell the coroner I would like them to repatriate his heart and any organ they have taken whole.

Today, in our garden, I see four robins. Maybe it's Jake, his best mate and his mum and dad.

I ask Jake's brother to come over and be with me whilst we go over the details of the funeral with the celebrant.

Martin, the celebrant, is a nice bloke. He looks a little bit like the monster from *The Goonies* but less lopsided.

He wants to know all the details of how I met Jake. I tell him we should avoid this as I was Jake's mistress for about seven years.

He asks all sorts of lovely questions just building up a profile of Jake. Bob and I relive the stories so they can be included in the service.

Music comes up. I have tried to listen to beautiful songs that were important to us both but they just break me. I don't want to make the funeral any worse than what I can already imagine it will be like. It took me a while to choose these gems.

Entrance music: 'Cuba' by Gibson Brothers. Jake and I went to Cuba on our honeymoon and went back several times. Jake fancied himself as a bit of a tour guide and endorser of all things Cuban

Halfway point: 'Glory Glory Man United'. Doesn't need an explanation. He was a massive fan.

To end: The funeral scene music from *Live and Let Die*. Jake always said when he goes, he wants to go out to that music from New Orleans with wailing black women following the coffin.

Martin doesn't blink an eyelid when I tell him my choices. Maybe he's seen it all before.

He says he'll write something up including a plan for times etc. He will liaise with the crematorium and confirm the date and time. Then he says I can then write the 'order of service.'

Martin also says it's nice that we have actually told stories about Jake. He says so many people tell stories about them and the whole thing can get quite selfish! I'm shocked at this.

Once Martin and Bob leave, my sister comes over.

Polly and I meet my sister-in-law Rachel in Spoons in town. She looks shattered but both look after me. We talk about Jake for most of the time. We aren't hammered. I can't handle it today. My head's all over the shop. I haven't told her that I had Bob over to go over the arrangements. She's too raw and she might not like that I asked Bob and not her.

✳✳✳

I am supposed to meet up with Jake's family this weekend but between them, they can't decide when or where and keep asking me to choose so I'm bailing.

My brave face has finally slipped. Maybe it's because 7th February seems so close. Something is shifting inside of me. I can't put my finger on it. I have been numb for weeks but now the numbness is subsiding and the hurt is becoming more and more painful.

Me, Polly and Dave go to the pictures to see the remake of *The Grudge*. How the fuck can there be a remake? The film's only a couple of years old. Just checked. It was made in 2004. FML, it's sixteen years old.

The film's pretty shit. Dave drops me and Polly at the pub opposite where I live and we go there for a wine or two as she's staying the night.

There is a little tiny fly, more like a midge, buzzing round my glass for ages. I look at Polly and she knows exactly what I'm thinking. It's clearly Jake so I don't try to shoo him away. I also keep watch to make sure he doesn't end up in my glass and drown.

There are two older men sitting at the table next to ours. Me and Polly are chatting quietly and I'm talking about Jake. And they invite us into their conversation which is about Meghan and Harry. We give them a short answer to be polite. I say I don't have an opinion on them, I'm not concerned by them and we should let them get on with it. They try to draw us back into their conversation and Polly keeps them talking. They probably think I'm a right miserable bitch. I am.

One of the chaps is particularly persistent and seems to quite like my sister. He says he doesn't believe me and Polly are sisters. Can't say I blame him as she's tiny and dark and I'm fat and blonde.

They offer us a drink. Being the polite girls we are, we accept. They bring over a couple of glasses of wine and then leave us to go out for a cigarette. When they come back, the louder chap asks us why we're out and what we're up to. I tell them we came out for a quiet drink as my husband died last month.

Strangely, if you just tell people outright, they soon fuck off. Probably felt awkward but they're actually very nice and give us both a cuddle and look quite upset but they leave us to it.

I chase the coroners again. I'm getting very nervous as the funeral is due in twelve days. The funeral directors have been chasing them as well.

I find it incredulous that the coroners must deal with the loved ones of the deceased and should also appreciate that everything needs to be to a timeline. They are so blasé about the whole thing.

It's making me so anxious and I can't think straight. Although I know Jake's family mean well, I sometimes think they believe I'm just sitting back and letting this all happen. It's just not in my control and when you're in a state of distress anyway, that's a hideous feeling.

I ask them if I can obtain an interim medical certificate as the results are still not back.

The doughnut from the coroners explains that he's had some results back from the post-mortem but he can't open them because the files encrypted.

He says he will call me tomorrow.

***

Chased the coroners again as nobody has called me and it's gone lunchtime.

He said he would chase the professors for an update and call tomorrow.

***

I go back to my GP this morning. I basically just break down.

I tell them I can't sleep. Every time I close my eyes, I'm taken back to Jake's resuscitation and my stomach sinks. I need something to get through the funeral at least. I've never suffered from mental health problems but I can honestly say I think I'm not going to make it through this. I don't know how people who genuinely don't have family or friends could handle this. I am lucky that at least I have people around me who are supporting me, even if I try to bat them away.

The doctor says I am suffering from PTSD. I finally get hold of some drugs. They prescribe me sertraline 50 mg which is apparently a low dose.

I still haven't heard back from the coroners.

I chase them again and speak to the doughnut that has been assigned to the case. He tells me that some of the reports are back. They say nothing untoward. He says he'll chase the professor for a conclusion and to get Jake's organs repatriated so Jake can finally be released to the funeral directors.

I explain to the doughnut that I am really struggling to deal with all of this and plead with him to chase the results.

He says he will call me tomorrow and says that he understands the time constraints.

I look up on Google (big mistake. Do not recommend) all about Jake's operation. Jesus, I wish I had realised the risk before he had it.

Would it have changed the outcome? I couldn't have stopped him from having it. If the aneurysm ruptured, he would have died immediately.

I think Jake played it all down to protect me. He knows I'd have worried even more than I already was, but when I think back, I think I knew how scared he was. I don't know how you can break an already broken heart.

✳✳✳

I am on my way to work and the funeral directors call me.

They let me know they have spoken to the coroners and that the funeral cannot go ahead next Friday.

They tell me my husband's heart will not be available for 7th February and consequently the coroner will not be able to sign off the medical certificate which is required for the funeral to go ahead.

I am going to lose my shit. I get to the office and try to call doughnut boy from the coroners office. It goes to voicemail, so I email him and ask him why the funeral directors know this before I do.

He was due to call me today.

I finally get hold of him and I'm like a deranged crow. I can't stop crying. I know I'm screaming at him. He explains that these delays are quite normal (it has now been over six weeks). I put the phone down on him as I am hysterical.

I receive an email from him and it says:

> *Please accept my apologies for not being in a position to proceed with the funeral arrangements which is due to pending histologies required by the pathologist to conclude their report and provide a cause of death.*

It was my intention to contact you in person with this information and not via the funeral directors.

I shall continue to chase the professor for the results. As soon as I receive an update, I shall contact you accordingly.

Oh, will you, doughnut? Just fuck off.

I have to let our family and friends know the funeral cannot go ahead. I let people know it is the fault of the wanky muppets at the coroners and that I can't confirm a new date as of yet.

No one understands quite how horrific it is to have to be responsible for something that you're not able to control all at the same time.

I arrange with the funeral directors, who are the only organisation that seem to give two shits, to reorganise Jake's funeral to 28th February 2020 and begin the task of letting people know.

All I can say is thank God for Facebook.

Fuck my life. That is all.

February 2020

I am finding it increasingly difficult to juggle my life. I am constantly battling not to cry. I am acting strong and I am hiding my utter despair to most people.

The constant calls and messages, although well-meaning, are at times too much.

I do not know what to do.

I feel Jake's family and even my own mum believe I am not pushing hard enough to get a decision from the coroners.

I do not think anyone quite understands how exhausting both mentally and physically just getting through a normal day is when you have a gigantic hole in your heart.

The thought of battling someone on the phone is terrifying. People have offered to step in but something inside of me needs to feel like I am in some kind of control. Plus, I saw the fucking lame email one of Jake's sisters sent to the coroner and no one can do a better job than me but it is literally fucking knackering.

I think the family believe I'm just waiting for the phone to ring. I have called or emailed the coroners every other day.

It feels too final to lay Jake to rest. In the headspace I'm in, I start to think that maybe this is payback. Maybe this is the reason everything is taking so long.

I look online today. I find several reports about the coroners office I am dealing with. They are not good. Local press stories from bereaved parents and spouses citing familiar excuses that I am seeing and hearing. I chase them up again.

Tomorrow would have been the funeral. Me, Polly and three of Jake's sisters decide to meet up in honour of Jake tomorrow and get wankered.

The doughnut sends me an email this morning:

> *Good morning Simone,*
>
> *My apologies for the delay in replying.*
>
> *On reviewing the case notes, I note the histology investigation has not been completed at this time. I shall chase the professor today to obtain an update and inform you accordingly.*
>
> *I trust you will find this satisfactory.*

I respond as follows:

> *Thank you, ***. No, I do not think this is satisfactory. It has now been eight weeks since my husband died.*
>
> *You have yourself admitted that the delay is not due to anything other than 'administration'. It is simply unacceptable.*

I am aware that this is not isolated to my husband's case. See above articles.

I attach a couple of articles that I found online.

Whilst I fully appreciate this is not your fault personally, some accountability needs to be accepted by your organisation.

I am not an unreasonable woman. I found you to be extremely compassionate in the early days. However, it has now got too much for me and the whole thing reeks of incompetence.

If a bona fide reason had been provided, it may have been less distressing but I am led to believe it is simply due to either lack of staff/time/management.

This is the single hardest time of my life and the coroners are certainly not making it any easier for me or my family.

I have cancelled my husband's funeral once — it was due to be today — and it will not be cancelled again.

I would therefore appreciate it if you could escalate this. If you are unable to confirm this, could you provide me with details of how I can do so myself.

All I want is to be able to say farewell for now to my partner of twenty-four years.

This is my first 'fuck you' response. It feels kind of empowering. Now I am off to get drunk.

Me and Polly head to Aldershite Spoons. Classy as ever.

The sisters are already there. We order red wine (bottle) for me, rose for Rachel, Patricia and Liz, and Prosecco for Polly.

Round One. Order food. Mainly nibbles. I consume a couple of deep-fried spicy prawns.

Liz manages to sweet talk the boys from the next table to give her a chicken wing. She refers to one of the lads as the one with the 'rose ning'. She means nose ring. It's going to be a good day.

Many, many bottles of wine and Prosecco are consumed.

I love fucking Spoons. All you posh fucks go and spend your cash in overpriced boutique bars but come the hell on. Bottle of Malbec, bottle of rose and a bottle of Prosecco: less than thirty quid. Goals.

We're quite loud and I don't think it's even lunchtime yet. Some of the other customers look a little nervy. Patricia's on form. She's flashed her knickers already. We move to a little booth (safer for surrounding patrons), eat some crisps and drink more wine.

After more knicker flashing and some Motown singing via YouTube on my mobile, Liz finally quits and vomits into the ice bucket holding the Prosecco. Luckily, the bucket was empty.

We're asked to leave by a member of staff. Seriously, we got kicked out of Spoons. If my life wasn't so fucking miserable, this moment would be priceless. Jake would be so proud.

We manage to get a lift from Liz's son. Once he is in town, he asks me where I live. Unfortunately, I can't remember but someone must have worked it out as Polly and I get home.

The following morning, Polly and me both feel delightful.

I read some messages on the group WhatsApp from yesterday. One of them is from Patricia messaging all of us at 4:30 p.m. to see if someone can pick her up. Mega LOLs.

We eat crisps all day, watch shit telly and drink copious amounts of diet coke. The other sisters are all feeling like shite.

I order myself a cushion with Jake's face on it. The picture I have chosen was taken at a wine bar in their outside space last July/August. He is pulling a face as he's 'vaping'. He gave up smoking as soon as he found out about the aneurysm. He looks like a bit of a cunt, but he's my cunt and I love him.

I'm only able to function by imagining me and Jake have split up. This is why he is not with me. No other reason. It works for a bit.

***

Monday comes and, on my way to work, I run into some random man who looks vaguely familiar. He says hello and asks how my rogue of a husband is. I almost fall to my knees, but I just start crying, shake my head and walk off. Poor bastard.

I make it to about lunchtime and leave the office.

When I get home, there are two letters for Jake: one from the opticians and one from Sandals offering some humdinger of a deal on a holiday.

I break down on the phone to my mum that afternoon and tell her I cannot get any answers from the coroners. I cannot cope with another cancelled funeral. She takes their number and says she will call them and fire a bullet up their arses.

She calls me back a little while later and says she got absolutely nowhere.

In fact, when she got shirty and explained my mental health was suffering, they did not show any empathy, so she told them she was not impressed and she was recording the conversation. Apparently, they just nervously laughed and said she should have told them earlier.

Fucktards.

I needed them to rebuff my mum because now I feel fucking insulted and decide I need to do something drastic.

I start to compile an official complaint to send to the CEOs of the hospital where Jake died and where he is currently (their emails are easily accessible from public records).

I copy in the coroners, the local press and my local MP. My email is a plea for help to get all of this sorted.

Good evening,

My husband Jake Forrester died on 12/12/2019 at *********** Hospital.

This was due to complications during a scheduled operation on 11/12 as he had an aortic aneurysm.

Following his death on 12/12, I contacted, as advised, the bereavement office at the hospital and was advised I would be contacted ASAP once the medical staff could establish the cause of death.

I was contacted by the coroners on 13/1 (after several calls to the hospital), four weeks after his death, to be advised there would be a post-mortem held on 17/1.

I advised the coroners on 20/1 that the funeral was planned for 7/2 and at no time was I told this could be an issue.

I was contacted on 20/1 by the coroners office to be advised that, following the post-mortem, a histology examination would be required.

They wanted to test my husband's spinal cord plus remove his heart and take samples of his liver, lungs and kidneys.

I chased the results on 27/1. I also asked if I may obtain an interim death certificate. I was advised the officer would chase the file, advising me he had part of the results back but couldn't open them as they were encrypted. He said he would call the following day.

I called again and was told he would chase the professor. I chased the day after and was told he would definitely call me back lunchtime on 30/1. I had made it clear at this stage I was struggling to deal with this and I needed some assurances I would be able to proceed with my husband's funeral.

On 30/1, the funeral directors called me to ask if I had heard anymore. They called themselves. They called me back to advise they had been told the funeral could not take place the following week as parts of the examinations hadn't been finalised.

I called the coroners and asked why they had told the funeral directors as opposed to myself and was assured they were going to let me know.

I cancelled my husband's funeral.

I chased again on 6/2 and was told on the day of my husband's original funeral date that the histology examination and results were still not complete and that they would let me know.

The emails sent and received are attached. I was told on 10/2 that it is still ongoing.

On each occasion I have spoken with the coroners officer, I have been told it is nothing sinister. It is simply issues with their administration. It has been mentioned on two occasions that because I would like my husband's organs repatriated this causes further delays. Each time this is mentioned I feel I am being blamed for this delay. I just want my husband to be whole.

I received a call from my contact at the coroners yesterday after sending the below email. He told me that unfortunately these delays are quite normal.

It has now been two months since my world collapsed. Whilst my contact at the coroners has been empathetic and I don't want to apportion blame on him directly as he has made it clear he can do very little other than to email the 'professors' involved but I can't seem to get through to anyone more senior.

He agreed to escalate matters to his senior and was due to email me a date next week that I could meet with them to discuss. I have not received any email as of yet.

My mother has called the coroners today and been met with a similar attitude of 'it's just how long it takes'. She called as a result of me sobbing on the phone to her as I just can't take much more. She may have been heavy handed but she's my mum — it should be expected and understood.

My own investigations into this particular coroners office came up with two cases last year where the delays were much less than my experience. The response last year from them was severe under resourcing. This appears to still be the case and lessons have not been learnt.

I was with my husband for twenty-four years and simply wish to say 'farewell for now' on the rescheduled date of his funeral. However, I am terrified I will once again be met with barriers.

I don't know what else to do. I have been advised to complain directly to my local authority and have copied in my local MP and also the local press.

I have also informed the hospital's press office as all these delays have led my husband's siblings to question why this hasn't been finalised and they talk of failings at the time of the operation. These are their thoughts, not mine.

If I need to redirect this, please, please let me know to whom as I am losing the will to go on.

Please help me.

Sincerely

Mrs Simone Forrester

I tell Jake I can't do this anymore. I tell him I wish I would get cancer and die. I know this is an incredibly selfish thing to say but I simply cannot cope on my own anymore. I ask

Jake if he wants me to end my life and be with him.

I ask him to give me a sign.

I tell him about this new virus that's knocking about in China and tell him that I hope some Chinese person comes over and licks me (non-sexually) so I get it and die. I ask him to please, please give me some strength as I am too tired to deal with fuck all.

✳✳✳

I must have cried myself to sleep again last night but I have woken up to two emails from the CEOs of the hospitals that have been sent before 8 a.m. this morning.

They have apologised and they are getting their senior staff onto it.

Throughout today, the emails and calls from representatives of the hospitals, registrars, council and lastly the coroners are relentless, but this is what was needed.

I am reassured the coroners will be contacting the professors at St George's and King's Hospital where the histology examinations are being held and they insist I will be called tomorrow.

I then get a call from the Serious Incident team at the hospital.

After enquiring who the hell they are, they explain they are a team who investigate an incident that occurred in relation to NHS-funded services and care resulting in unexpected or avoidable death.

This sends shockwaves through my whole being. Is someone to blame? Could this have been prevented?

She explains that Jake's death was reported to them last month. Once again, I'm the last to know.

There is to be an investigation on behalf of the trust that is in charge of the hospital and I understand the rationale behind the investigation is more of a 'lessons learnt' as opposed to any form of malpractice.

She tells me this will take a few months but will not hold up the funeral and she'll put it all in writing for me.

I make the calls to the family to let them know. I know they think there is someone to blame for Jake's death. I cannot think that way as imagining that this was preventable will just about finish me off.

I also thank Jake for giving me a bit of strength as I reckon he did. He would absolutely take no prisoners.

My cushion with his cunty face arrives and I absolutely bloody love it.

The coroners call me and tell me everything should be finalised tomorrow (incidentally, it is Valentine's Day tomorrow. Happy Valentine's Day to me).

That means I can register Jake's death and at least I know the funeral won't be cancelled.

They tell me his organs have been repatriated.

Unfortunately, in the email I receive from the manager at the coroners, he refers to Jake as Peter throughout. I ask him to please make sure they have the right person as it's

Jake not Peter.

FFS. Imbeciles.

I relay all of this to Jake's brother and sisters and get a phone call from Patricia this evening. She asks me if I am sure I don't what to go and see Jake in the morgue. I say absolutely not. I know how I want to remember him. Remembering it has now been over two months.

She asks if it may be wise that one of them goes to see him. For what purpose, I ask and she says they just want to check it really is Jake after they have fucked so many things up.

I tell her that's not helpful and frankly if it isn't going to be Jake at the funeral, what difference would that make to anyone?

I trust the funeral directors and all this scaremongering by the family is not making my life any more bearable. I don't understand why they ask such things. There are so many sisters. Why don't they discuss it together and realise by asking me they're just exasperating matters.

Maybe I'm being unfair. But I just don't need to hear this kind of thing.

Jake's brother has put a message up on our group WhatsApp saying he believes Jake is up there laughing at us all as we are all going nuts over all of these fuck ups.

I agree as that'd be Jake's style. He loved a wind up. I told him this morning that he was a fucker causing all this shit.

On another note, I sent an email to the council about four weeks ago explaining about Jake and asking if I was entitled to discounted council tax.

They send me an email. It says:

> *Dear Mrs Forrester*
>
> *Thanks for your email.*
>
> *I can confirm we have amended your account to reflect your husband passing away on 12/12/19. A single person discount has been awarded. A revised bill will follow.*

How pleasant. Not even a single word of condolence and it's from an actual human. This has made me rage.

Why are there so many motherfuckers around?

I feel like I need to purge on these people.

I take the cushion to bed and make a 'Jake' by putting his face on the pillow and his dressing gown in the bed as his body.

When I am in bed, I lay the arm of the dressing gown over my side like he's cuddling me. I also feel bad if I fart and the cushion is under the covers.

Bollocky Valentine's Day

I have bought a ridiculously expensive fillet steak to cook for 'us' tonight.

I cook it as I remember Jake used to say to cook it. He said:

- Make sure the steak is at room temp
- Hot griddle
- Oil and season the steak
- Once it's in the pan, *leave it*!
- Leave it to rest for at least five minutes once cooked

I do it by touch; about two minutes each side. I'm actually shitting myself when I'm cutting it. I feel like I would let Jake down if I've killed the steak. Judgy.

Incredibly, it is bloody perfect.

I wish I cooked more with Jake. He was so good. I was like Lady Muck just waiting to be served.

✳✳✳

Storm Dennis is upon us!

I hope it's nice and sunny and warm wherever Jake is. In my heart, I think it will be beautiful. Not so much white fluffy clouds and a big gold archway, more like a never-ending bar, fully stocked with good red wine and a roaring fire and leaded light windows… And nice loos.

I'm going out with Cora and Doug this evening.

They try to look after me. Cora was one of Jake's old flings. Sometimes she's a bit too familiar but I know she cares.

Caroline Flack has committed suicide. It's tragic. Cora is very judgmental about suicide. She has no idea how I feel as I hide it from everyone apart from Polly.

People should stop judging until they have walked in your shoes. One finger salute!

✳✳✳

The storm has fucked the garden up. There's shit everywhere and it's sodden.

Jake and me loved a storm. We saw a few phenomenal ones in the Caribbean.

I've done loads of things today but done nothing at the same time. I try so hard to push back the flashbacks of the resuscitation; they rip my heart out. It terrifies me referring to Jake in the past tense.

I speak to Jake and tell him about Caroline Flack. He won't recognise her as he wasn't in to reality TV but I ask him to get her a wine as she might be on her own and need looking after.

The funeral directors let me know today that the coroners will release Jake into their care tomorrow. I trust them and feel a little bit better.

When I think about how long it has been since Jake

went, I feel I have let him down as he's been here, there and everywhere for such a long time and I hate that.

I'm trying so hard to keep it together just to make it through to next Friday when I can lay him to rest but I even hate saying that. It makes it so final.

I still pretend he's not gone. Maybe he's gone into town or something and he'll walk through that front door any minute now loaded with non-essential food and drink.

Jake's family and some of his friends are pointing fingers at the hospital saying something wasn't right. No shit Sherlock, he fucking died. But it's making me stress even more. I can only reassure them that if this is the case, I will pursue it but right now, it's all I can do to get through the day. I genuinely didn't know that if your heart was already broken that it can get more broken, but it can.

Jake's now at last safe with the funeral directors. This gives me a bit of strength to carry on.

I'm definitely not quite right in the head. I keep asking Jake to show himself. I have always been obsessed with anything supernatural or paranormal. I even tell him that if he comes back in a zombie-like state (like Nick Frost in *Shaun of the Dead*), I'll keep him in the shed and look after him.

It is now one week and three days till the day I am dreading.

I think I may have meningitis or I've just fucked my neck up. I'm in agony.

Everything has been confirmed today about the funeral and the 'after party', and all the loose ends are tied up, but it is bittersweet as shit just got real and I can't pretend anymore.

∗∗∗

I'm in a strange place. Nothing seems real yet everything seems normal. It's so hard to explain.

I worry what I'm going to do after the dreaded day is over.

How do I even contemplate planning without Jake by my side?

I speak to my shrink today. I tell her how much I am dreading the funeral. She says it's usually the anticipation that is the worst, especially given the time that has elapsed in my case.

She says there is nothing wrong with wanting to celebrate the life Jake had. So, I am trying to concentrate on the last twenty-four years of our life together.

Some times were challenging but mostly we had a fantastic life together, especially after we got married in 2008.

I know he loved our life together. Mostly he enjoyed drinking wine and flying off to exotic places. He lived for sixty-two years and that's more than some but less than we all wanted.

I want to talk to him about all the shit we used to chat about: food, wine, holidays and how to best blow our money on all the things we loved.

Loved. I hate using past tense.

I'm off to get my eyebrows done as I look like a yeti. In other news, my meningitis has passed without death.

∗∗∗

Today, I meet up with a friend who calls me her best friend. I have known her since I was seventeen. We've been growing apart for years but on the plus side, she pays for lunch and includes a large glass of Malbec for me.

I'm trying to get through to next Friday by remembering all the fantastic things Jake and I did together, but it hurts so much. I think to myself that one day we will be doing things together but in a different place and not just yet.

I speak to one of Jake's sisters today. She's an alcoholic. She was very close to Jake and she is also very isolated where she lives, nowhere near any of us, and that must make it even harder. At least my family and friends aren't far away.

∗∗∗

Mum and Dad come over today. I can see the pain etched on their faces. I don't want them to worry about me cracking up. They're getting on and it pains me to see them suffer. I know they were always content in the knowledge that whatever was going on, Jake and I were so happy. This gave them comfort and now they're scared.

I tell them this and tell them I will be okay. I'm doing this for their sake only as I'm definitely not okay. I think they buy it.

I think they must be waiting for me to cook them something extravagant. Jake cooked them fabulous lunches every single time they came to see us, without fail.

Unfortunately, they get bacon rolls from me as I can't live up to Jake's skills in the kitchen, plus I really can't be fucked.

✶✶✶

Just before I leave work today, a good friend of mine Lola messages me to say she has got something to give me when she sees me at the funeral on Friday.

She says she wants me to see it before she gives it to me as she doesn't want me to be overwhelmed and asks if she can send me a picture of said gift. I ask her to message me once I'm home so I can prepare myself!

I get home, stick my head out of the stable door, light a fag and give Lola the green light.

She sends me a picture of a beautiful drawing of Jake and I. It's a replica of a picture I posted on Facebook announcing the news. It's just lovely and makes me cry but happy/sad tears.

I get an email after chasing BA for my refund for those flights, saying can I call them again. Fuck off.

I feel numb at the moment. I'm just plodding through until Friday. I don't want to crash and burn.

I'm getting concerned about Jake's son. He has 'gone dark'. He isn't that close to the rest of the family for no reason other than he does usually keep himself to himself. I think he is struggling and I know Jake would want me to look out for him and I've made a promise that I will.

I ask Jake to give David a bit of strength as I don't think he's as strong as he makes out. I also tell Jake that he shouldn't worry about David as I'll look out for him.

It's the hideous day tomorrow.

At least this morning when I wake up, I think I will be with Jake tomorrow.

I will never ever say goodbye though. Never.

The more I think about tomorrow, the more I am terrified.

I've asked Jake's two nieces to look out for David tomorrow. I know Polly will be at my side all day. I don't know what I'd do without her.

My lovely hairdresser is coming to do my hair tomorrow morning. She offered to do it for me as she can't get to the funeral due to childcare. At least my barnet will look good as I'm damn sure the rest of me will look like fucking shite.

I've asked everyone to come with a 'pop' of red in their attire tomorrow.

I'm wearing black jeans, a black jumper and jacket and some brand new ridiculously expensive wine-coloured boots from Hobbs.

This coronavirus thing appears to be spreading across the world; even people here are getting concerned about it. My brother-in-law says he'll be handing out bottles of Corona at the 'after party' tomorrow and reckons they'll come with a public health warning

Jake's alcoholic sister calls me this evening to say she isn't coming tomorrow. She can't handle it. I don't mind and I do understand. Frankly, it's probably for the best. She has sent me £100 to go behind the bar for tomorrow and I am grateful. I don't expect anyone to pay for anything but it's nice that she has done this.

I've also said that his estranged sister is welcome as long as she realises the day is not about her. It's about Jake and Jake alone. I had cut her out of my social media as she is just too narcissistic.

The Day

I had a dream last night that the coroners called me and told me Jake was the original carrier of this coronavirus and he'd started an epidemic.

He'd love that. World domination — check.

I get a message from Polly this morning. It just says, 'I've got this shit, so lean on me, feeling like a proper boss lady.' I love her so much.

My hairdresser does my hair. It does look good and she takes my mind off the impending doom.

Mum, Dad, Polly and Dave turn up about an hour before the funeral kicks off.

Poor old Dad's wearing a suit and looks so bloody uncomfortable. I feel for him.

How to start the day of your husband's funeral?

Get 'your hair did' and start drinking shots of cherry flavoured Polish vodka.

Excellent start. Polly and my mum (WTF) partake as well.

I chain smoke for the hour before we have to leave.

Dave drives us to the crematorium and I can feel Polly's eyes boring into me. She's realised she's likely to have to prop me up today. Now I feel okayish. For some reason, I am obsessively reapplying my eyeliner in the car. Jake used to cringe if I did this in a moving vehicle (I can't drive so don't panic).

Once we get to the crematorium, we head towards the meeting room. It's quite big and it is the waiting room before we go into the main room for the service.

It is incredibly daunting. We are the first there. I feel like we're preparing for a macabre party and am nervous nobody will turn up. I feel quite sick.

I haven't really prepared for this day. It has been looming for so long now. I know I have purposely avoided thinking about the actual day as it is still too much to even comprehend.

People begin to arrive. A few old friends from various workplaces etc. Then some of Jake's family and then lots of people I don't know very well but who know Jake. Within a few minutes, the room has filled up and I'm finding myself 'doing the rounds'.

One of my old work friends just says to me, 'Oh, Simone,' and looks at me with so much pity that it brings me close to tears. 'I'm fine,' I say.

The celebrant comes and gives me the nod that we all need to go into the room where the service is being held.

I walk in and I can hear the chosen tune of 'Cuba' and that makes me smile.

The room is filling up and there is light chat.

I am sitting between Polly and Mum. Dad is next to Mum and Jake's kids are next to him. All of us in the front. Jake's siblings go to sit behind me and I ask them to sit in the front row on the opposite side. They say they want to support me but I insist they sit on the other side right at the front. It's where they should be.

I am okay. I am looking round and I am pleased there are plenty of people. I can't imagine how you'd feel if nobody was there to pay their respects.

I then notice the coffin. I'm not sure why I don't notice it before. It has clearly been there all the time but I have only just clocked it. I knew it would be there so I don't know why it is such a shock.

I tell Polly and she holds my hand. My heart is beating fast. I feel kind of 'fizzy'. It is difficult to explain. It's like I'm not really experiencing this but watching it through somebody else's eyes.

The service starts and I reconnect. The celebrant is lovely. He talks about Jake like he knows him, acknowledging all of the family and friends and really capturing Jake's personality.

He really does well but I suppose that's because we supplied him with some brilliant anecdotes.

Midway through the service, they play 'Glory Glory Man United' and people get up to leave gifts on the coffin.

For anyone other than family, they'd think that maybe what is being placed on the coffin is disrespectful but again his family represent him so well. It is all about the piss take. He would have loved that.

First on is a pair of silver platforms (Jake apparently strutted his stuff in a similar pair during the seventies).

Next go on a tin of baked beans. Jake was the oldest still at home when his brothers and sisters were younger. He was left to cook for them when his mum was at work and his dad was down the pub. Apparently it was mainly beans on toast — he got better.

A packet of fags, a Motown CD, a bottle of red wine and a Man U shirt. All self-explanatory.

I place our expired passports and his favourite picture of me on top of the coffin.

The gifts break the sadness for a second.

After this, the celebrant reads a poem called 'The Measure of a Man'. I didn't choose it. Poetry is not my strong point but it is quite nice.

He then finishes with a roundup of Jake's life and how sad we all are to lose him.

Jake's son is sobbing quietly. I want to go to him but I know that would draw more attention to his distress and his step-sisters are looking after him.

The voile curtains around the coffin start to close and the closing music (remember the New Orleans jazz funeral march?) starts to play, and it plays and plays for what seems to be hours. It never starts getting jazzy, just a monotonous blurge of trombones. It is supposed to get lively but it doesn't. That was supposed to be the happy music. FFS!

I can hear Jake's two nieces giggling behind me.

The celebrant apologises to me and says he played it a few days ago and it was correct and he doesn't know what has happened. Sums up the last few weeks really. Pretty sure Jake would be laughing.

I take a deep breath and walk outside.

I didn't realise I would need to stand outside of the ceremony room and shake everyone's fucking hands and talk to them. Apparently, it's just what you do. I was all for legging it back to the car and getting to the pub sharpish.

It's drizzling. My hair better not go frizzy. I send Mum and Dad to the car and Polly stays just slightly behind me.

People say some lovely things but I only hear parts of what they're saying — it's not the vodka, I've sobered up by now — it's just like the teacher speaking to Charlie Brown.

Jake's ex-wife says something to me. I know it's nice but it hasn't registered. I just say thank you to anyone that says anything to me and I'm fine.

Finally, everyone leaves and I hug the celebrant and thank him. He discreetly gives me a bag of items that were left on the coffin that can't go with Jake: nothing flammable or that would cause an explosion, so the silver platforms are mine now.

Small things like this take you back to reality and make you face what is really happening inside that cordoned off area where my husband's body now is lying

***

After Party

I had asked the pub to pop a chalk board up that says 'JAKE'S PISS UP' outside the area we have cordoned off. They didn't let me down. People might think I am being flippant by making a joke out of this but I am not. I just want to represent Jake as best I can and socially drinking was a big factor in his life.

When I get to the pub, it's already quite full with people I do and don't know.

The manager of the pub shows me the table with the wine and Prosecco and tells me he has opened up a tab to the sum of £300 so everyone can have a drink.

He says he will bring out the food in stages but will start straight away. Maybe he can judge what kind of event this is likely to be.

I mingle. I am given a bottle of Malbec from a girl I used to work with who paid for it over the phone from the pub with her best wishes and apologies that she can't make it.

That's mine now.

Wherever I go and whomever I am talking to, I am given a glass of wine.

My mum has seated herself in the corner and is being looked after by Natalie. She asks for a gin as she obviously can't make it to the bar herself. Lazy bitch.

All I asked of my parents is to try to talk to the people who have come to pay their respects. I didn't ask for anything else, just for them to do that. My sister is talking to everyone. But Mother is sat there right in the corner and is provided a large gin by someone.

My dad looks so sad. He doesn't like crowds and he's not the kind of person to 'work the room'.

He hangs out with my sister's husband and Greg. I am kind of okay with that, but I feel Mum could make more of an effort.

Jake's youngest daughter holds up a glass of red in one hand and a glass of Prosecco in the other exclaiming she's drinking her husband's drink as he is driving. That's not really the idea, but she's family so I let it pass.

I am standing talking to one of Jake's sisters and Cora comes up to join in the chat. She introduces herself to Rachel and by way of introduction she says, 'I was the Simone before Simone.' I note Doug is nowhere to be seen otherwise I am pretty sure she wouldn't have said that. It is absolutely not appropriate and Rachel says, 'There was no one before Simone,' immediately squashing that bullshit. I smile to myself as Rachel one hundred percent has my back and is now looking at Cora like she is a piece of shit on her shoe.

Best I leave, I think and I work my way around the room. I speak to people I've not seen for a few years and we talk about Jake.

My sister is by my side constantly.

Cora is intermittently sticking bits of food in my mouth and tells me I should shut down the bar now as it's been open for too long. She's worried we'll go over budget.

I needn't have worried. The manager stopped it at exactly £300. I pay it and miraculously remember my pin number for my card.

There is Motown playing in the background (another request of mine).

It is starting to get louder. All of Jake's family are sat in a semi-circle reminiscing. To anyone looking in who is not in the clique, it would look pretty scary but I love them.

My goddaughter Louise, who will be eternally twelve in my eyes, is at the bar and tilts her hand back and forth indicating can she buy me a drink — that makes me laugh. She's nineteen now. I shake my head pointing at the several full glasses of wine I seem to have accrued.

I don't know how long I've been here but I'm flagging. I am chain smoking outside with Charley, Louise and Lola and there is always a full bloody glass of wine in my hand.

I speak to my boss and call someone we work with a fucking cunt and they laugh. I'm clearly on form.

Mum and Dad leave. I am relieved and now only the hardened crew are here.

Then something switches.

Someone tells me Jake's youngest daughter has been slagging off her father, telling anyone who will listen that he was a shit dad. It enrages me but I can't react.

I also take note that she has uploaded a fucking Instagram video of her at her own father's wake talking about her new hair colour.

I tell one of Jake's nieces that I need to do something to sort my head out.

I'm whisked out of the pub into another of Jake's niece's husband's car. We drive out of the pub car park and into a side road near to the pub. He pulls out a wrap and sprinkles me out a large line of white powder.

I take a line of coke. FFS.

Instantly I feel better. He gives me a little package and that's me sorted now.

I have to tell you this is the first time I have taken cocaine for approximately twenty years. Jake hated drugs. I, however, am a fan of recreational use, but I stopped two decades ago as he would've disowned me. Obviously, it is appropriate to take it at your husband's fucking funeral.

I don't know what I'm thinking. Well, I'm not thinking. That's the point, I suppose.

I speak to David who looks lost and I tell him I love him (must be the drugs) and that it is going to be okay.

The rest of the day/evening passes by in a high/low stupor. I don't think anyone realises I'm off my nut on anything other than wine and if they do, I really don't give a flying fuck.

I recall going into the ladies' with Jake's niece. We do a couple of lines off the loo seat. Classy.

I'm sat with Jake's eldest grandson who's telling me about all the drugs he's done as he's depressed and I try to get him to talk about his music.

I've heard him sing and play the guitar and he's very good. He's sat between me and his mum. He's offloading on me telling me all his problems but I'm okay with it as it's making me less wired.

All of a sudden, Natalie says to his mum maybe it's

better he doesn't offload on me as it's not the right time or place. She a hundred percent means well and is looking out for me.

It kicks off and Jake's eldest daughter is crying with anger at Natalie who leaves the pub, swiftly followed by Greg. He then comes back and says he's sorry but he's got to find her.

I try to placate Jake's eldest daughter, and we decide we should leave this place and go to the pub opposite as it's mainly stragglers now.

We go over the road.

I remember red wine and shots are ordered along with pizza and chips (I think).

Jake's grandson offers me some coke or speed or something, I don't know what it is. He gives me a little baggie and off I go to the bogs. Unfortunately, I lose said baggie as I'm so completely out of it.

I think he thinks I'm lying but I'm not. You know what it's like when you're off your nut. It's like trying to open your front door with your key. You can never do it right. You either drop the key or miss the keyhole or go to the wrong house (no?).

He's waiting for me outside the loos. Jake's eldest daughter, for some reason, is also there and I stupidly confess what's going on. No idea why. Maybe guilt?

Smart move. Now it really kicks off.

My sister is now aware I have taken coke. She's absolutely raging, asking me where I got it from and saying she's not cross with me she's angry as nobody should've given it to me in my vulnerable state. I try to explain it was a hundred percent my idea. She's not buying it.

Jake's grandson, who by the way is twenty-one, has now fucked off and done a runner. Next thing I know, old gobby chops (Jake's youngest daughter) is kicking off at my sister about flirting with Beth's husband? WTF.

It's definitely time to go home, which thankfully is less than a five-minute walk away, although it takes about fifteen minutes as I am well and truly wonky.

The Aftermath

I can't tell you how guilty I feel at doing coke last night. Jake would've gone nuts.

I feel utterly lost and empty. I ask Jake if he can help me, but I think he'd be disgusted.

Meanwhile, I pick up my clothes from last night to put in the wash and it appears I have wet my pants and feel like shit.

I go to bed early. I wake up in what I think is the early hours of the morning. Except I haven't as it's not even 11 p.m.

Literally fuck my life.

March 2020

I feel so bad, just a real sad feeling and I feel like I let Jake down. Nobody knows what happened apart from Polly and the two girls. That's enough.

It's beginning to dawn on me Jake's not coming home and I really don't fancy a life without him. He's so loved not just by me but by so many.

I'm still hoping this virus from China comes and gets me and takes me out of my misery.

Polly messages me to see how I am. I tell her she needs to come over and turn me over in bed as I think I might get bed sores if I don't move soon. I feel like a massive pig in a blanket.

***

I cannot face work today. I had every intention of going in but I know somebody will no doubt ask me about the funeral and I can't handle it.

The news is all about this Covid shit. Apparently, it could cause some real harm. Better not turn up before my Ocado delivery this evening as I've ordered snacks.

I ordered some light bulbs for the spotlights under our

kitchen cupboards. I did it via Amazon. Miraculously, I ordered the right ones. Achievement.

The SI team email me and advise me to list some questions I would like for them to present to the board of professionals who will review Jake's case. Bleugh. Just thinking about it knots up my guts.

I love Jake more and more each day. How is that even possible?

***

I am feeling a bit stronger today.

The company I work for are supporting me and are not pushing me to do full days. We've agreed for me to do 9:30 to 3:30 but to be flexible with it. Thank God for their support. I've read some horror stories recently about some companies, especially small businesses, who simply aren't equipped with dealing with grief.

This evening, I am attempting to cook another of Jake's inspired meals. I am trying to stop eating beige foods and introduce some goodness into my life.

This reminds me of some of the things the celebrant said about Jake at the funeral. He spoke about Jake's cooking and the fact he was known for his love of platters.

These were platters of all types of food, a bit like tapas but Jake style.

One of my favourites was gorgonzola stuffed mushrooms with roasted tomatoes, sourdough bread and fancy sausages with balsamic glaze. Sounds poncy, I know.

He used to 'cunt things up'. This involved adding his spin on all foods. This is why I failed to reach my goal of being a size 12. I'm not greedy. Well, I am. A size 12 would be bloody marvellous. Currently my beige food eating is not going to help me achieve this.

I have started to think that Jake would not be angry with me.

I have spoken to Beth about the hideous events of the funeral and she said to me that she doesn't know what she would've taken if she'd have lost her husband. She doesn't blame me at all. She's angry with her son for giving me drugs but actually it might've worked out okay as he is now getting some help for his mental health.

Always an unseen benefit after being peddled cocaine at your late husband's funeral by his eldest grandson.

✳✳✳

Today, I have emailed the Serious Investigation team at the trust and asked them various questions about the sequence of events during and after Jake's operation.

Questions such as:

Why did it take so long to finally locate Jake?

Why did nobody contact me when things started to go wrong?

Why did they go ahead with the operation when they located multiple clots in his legs?

Why did his heart fail when he'd previously been told his heart was okay?

What caused the extremely high levels of potassium in his body?

I was informed on 12th February it was reported as a serious incident in January, so why was I not informed until 12th February?

Jake was conscious when I was with him in ICU. He was in a considerable amount of pain and kept trying to sit up. Why was he not given something to sedate him rather than be writhing in pain? He was given some pain relief after I asked the nurses to provide him with something.

Once he was given pain relief, he began retching and I advised the nurses and they supplied him with a bowl. Why wasn't he sedated?

Was Jake paralysed and if so, what caused this?

I was given the option of seeing Jake whilst he was being resuscitated. I went. This was the biggest mistake I made as I now have to take medication for PTSD. What was the rationale behind being asked if I wanted to see him?

They have advised that a meeting with the panel selected for Jake's investigation will be this week and she will present our questions and then come back to me. She said it is likely to take some time.

I have promised Jake that if somebody is accountable, I will pursue it and get some answers.

I don't want this to be anyone's fault. Why would I?

Imagine if this could have been prevented… I don't think I could live with that.

His family are gunning for the operating team or the hospitals. I get it, I really do but I simply can't think that way. I now know why they say anger is part of grieving. His family are angry but I'm not. I am devastated, shocked, desperate and sad but I am not angry.

It has not stopped raining for days. I have asked Jake to stop it from raining although it is suited to my fucking mood.

It's sunny today. I thank Jake.

Work's not too bad. I get through it like some kind of semi-functioning loon. I can tell people are avoiding me, but I can't blame them. I'd definitely avoid me.

A couple of weeks ago, I was going through Jake's mobile and I found a picture he'd taken of a sign in a little antiques shop near our house. It says, 'NOBODY GETS OUT SOBER' in a kind of road sign style. Jake must've liked it.

I visit the shop and show this nice old boy the picture and explain my husband took a photo of it as he liked it. The old boy says he'll try to order me one and says Jake should've got it there and then as they flew out.

I make a chilli tonight. I use proper beef chunks like Jake used to as he said it was more authentic. I don't follow a recipe and just bung it in like he did. Smells good.

I am meeting one of his sisters tomorrow for lunch.

***

I walk into town and it really does remind me of Jake. We were always here.

I meet Patricia outside M&S and we walk to The Star. I order a large glass of Malbec, may as well start as I mean to go on. Patricia orders a glass of rose and when the girl behind the bar takes a half-opened bottle from the fridge, Patricia insists that she opens a fresh one.

We have a couple of large ones and off we trot to the Italian. They sit us downstairs. Reckon they can tell there's no way we'll be able to get up and down those stairs pretty soon.

We don't eat a lot but manage at least two bottles of Primitivo red. I think I try to eat some olives and a carbonara.

We left the restaurant around 4 p.m. and for some reason, I decided to change my ringtone on my mobile to a beep… Fuck knows.

I remember going into Sainsbury's absolutely steaming, buying all sorts of snack-based items.

I find out later that Polly was calling me to make sure I was okay. I forgot she had put a tracking app on my phone. She was tracking me leaving town and I was going all over the shop.

As I'd missed a thousand calls from Polly, she then panicked and made Dave drive her to mine to make sure I was home. I was.

She tells me that she thought she saw me going into a KFC. She knows I like a chicken nugget.

I remember Polly leaving and I was crying in my back garden. It transpires that I was talking to my elderly neighbour in my garden and pouring my heart out. Cringe.

Then I try to take some pills but bottle it and speak to one of Jake's sisters, Rachel, who talks me out of it. Then two hours later, I am messaging Polly telling her I am fine and she's not to worry.

Lately, I am either sober or steaming. There is absolutely no in between.

✳✳✳

I get a letter though this morning from the surgeon who performed Jake's op (clearly, I hate him). He offers his condolences and asks whether I would feel it would be beneficial to come and see him to talk through what happened. He says some relatives find this helpful in terms of grieving and that it may help.

I'm not sure how I feel about speaking with him. I am nervous that if I speak to him face-to-face, I won't hold it together. Plus, do I really want to give him the heads up about all the shit that's going on with the SI and the coroners? In the end, my mind is made up. He signs off saying to contact his PA to arrange an appointment, which kind of takes all of the empathy away.

I don't expect him to give me his mobile number or anything and I appreciate he is a busy guy but it just irks me that his letter ends so impersonally.

***

Work are starting to take this COVID-19 seriously. I get a message from Lola who's not well at all. She's been taken to hospital with possible Covid or pneumonia. I let work know and immediately they are trying to send me home as it could be the dreaded virus and Lola was at the funeral.

Funny enough though, once I let them know that if I need to go home a couple of others will need to as they too were at the funeral, they recalculate the days and I get to stay at work.

Fingers crossed for Lola. Not sure at the moment what would be worse: Covid or pneumonia.

Before Jake was diagnosed with the aneurysm, we were due to go on holiday with Greg and Natalie for their fiftieth birthdays to Benidorm. Don't judge. It was for the LOLs.

We made all the arrangements around three months before he was diagnosed. Once he was told about the aneurysm, we asked about flying and the consultant said it wasn't safe to fly. So, we unfortunately had to let our friends down. They completely understood but we were so pissed off.

We booked the hotel through a well-known online booking firm and the flights via, again, a very well-known airline. We paid for the hotel and Greg and Natalie paid for the flights and it was approximately £600 for each couple.

Once we knew Jake couldn't fly, we cancelled our booking for the hotel with the holiday company, advising them of the circumstances. We didn't push for our money back. All we wanted was to make sure Greg and Natalie could stay there with no issues as we'd booked it as a group booking. They confirmed that they could amend the booking and that was that.

The airline said they would transfer our flights for up to a year, which was okay with us as we were bound to go away again.

On the day Greg and Natalie flew out, they called us to say they had arrived but they'd been refused entry as the booking was in Jake's name and they claimed they knew nothing of the cancellation.

In a nutshell, Greg and Natalie had to pay again for another room. This is despite the two rooms we booked for the four of us were clearly not in use!

I contacted the holiday firm and they claimed they had made the amendments and advised the hotel but it was at the hotel's discretion if they accepted the cancellation and the rebooking under the new lead passenger's name.

Motherfuckers. They didn't tell us this.

Jake made it his mission to get the money back from

the holiday company.

We got half the money back and we paid Greg and Natalie the cost of the new room.

Today, we got the money back from the airline as well after I contacted them to say I wouldn't be travelling for a while and explained about my loss. They weren't too bad to deal with.

Jake'd be so happy.

Everything I do, I try to do it like he would do it. I can be quite ruthless when I put my mind to it.

✳✳✳

For fuck's sake. I've just gone to put on the same jeans I wore when I was out with Patricia at the weekend and notice they've got a massive scuff mark on the knee.

That can only mean one thing. I fell over on Saturday. Bollocks. I bet that's how my neighbour found me on Saturday evening and got into my garden.

I cannot be trusted.

I receive the following email from my representative of the SI team:

> *Unfortunately, yesterday the decision was made to delay the panel meeting due to the pressures on the trust caused by the COVID-19 situation.*
>
> *I am really sorry about this and will do everything I can*

to reorganise it as soon as possible.

I will keep you informed of the situation but would like to assure you that all of your questions will be raised by myself when the panel is able to convene.

I can't say I am too surprised. Covid is hardly their fault.

I chase the coroners again. It is now almost ten weeks since I lost Jake and the cause of death has yet to have been established. I am unsure if this is connected to the Serious Investigation. It makes you paranoid.

I get the following response from the coroners:

Your husband's death is still under investigation and we are just waiting for a medical report (histology of spinal cord) from King's College Hospital.

We have been advised that the report is to be expected within the next two weeks. Upon receipt, the report will be forwarded to the pathologist in order to prepare the post-mortem report, which will then need to be reviewed by the coroner in order to decide on the next steps. It is difficult to given an exact timeline but it could take another four to six weeks.

My colleague **** ***** is the officer looking after Jake's case, but I am also part of the investigation team and one of us will be in touch once the pathologist has provided the cause of death.

Had enough today.

Then the dude from the antiques shop calls me to say he's got me that sign! Yay!

I go and pick it up. It is massive.

I tell the chap why it is so important to me and I think he's taken aback.

As I'm walking back home with the sign, I resist the urge to try to pole vault with it, it's that big.

Can't face my neighbour so I pop a note through her door saying I'm sorry if I was a knob on Saturday.

Jake's eldest sister announces she thinks she's got Covid, but then admitted she thinks it's just a cold. Ever the drama queen.

***

I am going to pick Jake up today from the crematorium. I am morbidly excited. I keep imagining that once he is at home with me, I will be able to communicate with him and that he will haunt me.

I just want him home with me. My boss takes me to the crematorium.

The box is actually rather lovely. It's varnished pine with a plaque on it, but it is so heavy.

I had been comparing it to when we got our cat's ashes. I didn't think it would be so much heavier, which is absolutely ridiculous comparing a cat that weighed about seven pounds to Jake who weighed about twelve stone.

Once I'm home, I sit him next to me on the settee.

I have a bottomless Prosecco brunch booked at The Mandalay tomorrow with Lola, Trixie and Donna.

I predict carnage.

Lola messages me to say she's still not feeling too well so she's bailing. I'm sure the three of us can still do some damage.

∗∗∗

Trixie comes and picks me up just before lunch, courtesy of her son, to take us to the hotel. We have two hours to drink as much Prosecco as we can.

I am a professional. I can do this shit.

The hotel where the brunch is being held is almost completely empty. Must be this Covid shit. Should we actually be taking this more seriously?

We tell, actually, I tell the waiter to come fill our glasses up every nine minutes to get optimum value for money. We 'fill up' on tiny sandwiches and mini cakes.

We end up going on a mini pub crawl after the brunch. I clearly don't know when to stop.

I must remember Polly has fitted me with a tracker.

I have absolutely no recollection of getting home.

I look through my phone at gone 11 p.m. (I went out at 12:30 p.m.) and Polly messaged me at 19:22 telling me she can see I'm home. She messaged again at 19:50 saying she imagines I'm asleep, and again at 21:44 asking me to message her so she knows I'm safe.

I message her when I wake up at 23:18 still in my clothes.

✳✳✳

I feel absolutely sparkling today. My head is banging. I look through my phone and there are a shit load of pictures on it. Some of them are quite good but some of them are very bad.

Trixie tells me the three of us went to a pub after we left the hotel and I was drinking a lot of red wine. I think I remember that.

Trixie and I were wearing (almost) matching red leopard print dresses and we look a bit demented. Then apparently Donna left to go home and Trixie and I went to Turtle Bay for cocktails as we needed them, of course.

I was banging my head (softly) on the table at Turtle Bay. I really hope nobody was taking too much notice of us.

Trixie then said she was worried about me as I was weaving in and out of the road on the way home chucking my handbag all over the place. Polly also confirmed this and said the tracking app had me weaving in and out. Thankfully she wasn't too concerned as she knew I was with Trixie who'd look after me!

Trixie got me home, chucked me inside the house and

said I had a little stumble. Then she left and went to The White Hart with her son for a glass of vino. She's probably exhausted after looking after me.

Apparently, I flashed my pants through my opaque tights at her.

How pleasant for her.

***

St Patrick's Day

In honour of Jake, we arranged for some of the family to meet up with Polly and I.

We also invited a few friends but due to the ever more concerning Covid, some of them have bailed.

Me and Polly are not taking Covid seriously at all. Clearly, we just want to get drunk.

There ends up being just seven of us and we meet in a pub in town. It is so strange. I have never been out on St Patrick's night and sat in an empty pub. We are the only ones in the pub. This is a place which is frequented by a rugby crowd, so to see it empty is bizarre.

We all greet each other touching via elbows. Rachel gives us hand sanitiser.

We have a glass of wine then off we trot to the Indian. Fuck's sake, that's empty too. It's so odd.

The owner greets me and offers me his condolences and

then gives us all a squirt of hand sanitiser and gives us some starters on the house in honour of Jake (we frequented the place often) plus a nice bottle of Malbec for me. Here I go again.

He tries to get the restaurant's sound system working and play a bit of Motown at our request rather than the Bollywood style music that's usually playing. It doesn't work, so Sean switches his mobile to loud speaker and plays a bit through his phone (needs must). We get fed and get drunk.

The owner gets the girls to gather round him. He's being a big Asian flirt, and we take some pics. Sienna points at the elaborate belt he is wearing. It's hideous, gold and gaudy with what looks like a clock face on it. It's kind of Liberace-esque. It's also very near his penis. This encourages Sienna to shout, 'cocky watch' and piss herself laughing. She is hilarious.

It's probably a good job we're the only ones in the restaurant.

The food is lovely but as usual, I eat fuck all and tuck in to the wine. Liz gets first dibs on the doggy bags and pretty much clears us all out.

The girls pay for my drinks and dinner and then five of us — me, Polly, Sienna, Ashleen and Rachel — head off to the classiest joint in town: Spoons.

A bottle of rose for Sienna and Rachel, a bottle of red for me and Ashleen, and Polly comes back with six shots of sambuca as she can't face any more wine. That's my girl.

Me and Polly head off back to mine, drunk but laughing. I decide to have a little lie down in the mews I have to walk down to get to my house. No reason, just can't be bothered to walk anymore.

I must make this the last time I get sideways. I'm a liability.

***

Jake's Birthday

I'm sad today and my heart just won't mend.

I knew today would be hard.

People bang on about 'the firsts' in grief. I can't imagine ever not feeling sad.

We would definitely have been on holiday somewhere if everything was 'normal'.

We made it 'our thing'. For birthdays, special occasions, etc., we always went on holiday somewhere. Last year, it was New York.

I pop to Waitrose today. No meat, no tins, no fresh veg, no pasta or potatoes. It feels a bit like I am in *The Handmaid's Tale*. Blessed be thy fruit. Luckily, there's loads of Easter eggs, so that will do nicely.

I really need Jake right now. I know he would tell me what to do. As in, should I being going out? Should I worry about Covid?

I'm waiting for a Boris update on Covid. Jake would've hated being told what to do, but he'd also know that I'd be a little bit excited.

I'm making a platter tonight: Roquefort cheese, focaccia bread, salami and olives plus baked cherry toms. Guess those items are not high on people's lists for stock piling.

I feel like shit. I just want him with me.

I refrain from drinking this evening as I decide I need to be sober. Angel.

Boris updates the country. We are all being locked down. Looks like I am working from home for the foreseeable.

Pubs, restaurants, etc. are closing from tomorrow due to Covid. I guess I was lucky I could get as much in over the last couple of weeks before this shit show really reared its ugly head.

✳✳✳

Mum and Dad come over. We know this will be the last time for a while as they'll be shielding. Polly comes over too. We go to the local little shop down the road and try to stock up on some tins etc. for the olds. We buy a massive tin of Heinz beans just for LOLs. It is 'catering' size, plus get them some biscuits, tinned toms, pasta sauces, plus a bottle of scotch for Dad. Essentials.

Me and Polly also buy a ridiculous amount of noodles,

tinned shite, crisps, biscuits, chocolate and squash. Better to be prepared just in case.

Blessed be the fruit, under his eye.

I make Mum and Dad a 'naanwich' which is basically a naan sandwich with tandoori chicken, raita and mango chutney plus salad.

Dad gives it a nine out of ten. I am honoured. I know he wouldn't give me a ten out of respect for Jake as Jake was the best cook ever.

When they go, I watch a little video of me and Jake in NYC last year on St Patrick's Day. We're drinking wine in an absolutely heaving bar. It was such a good night.

That night in NYC, when we got back to the hotel, Jake went downstairs for a cigarette. When he came back to our room, he told me he'd been approached outside the hotel and asked if he wanted to score some crack. He declined. Good times. How can things change so dramatically?

Well, 2019 ended pretty fucking terribly and 2020 isn't going much better.

Arrange a video call with Lola and Trixie (aka the Lollipops) this evening. Is this the extent of our social life now?

***

I'm now getting a bit nervous. Shit's getting real. How the hell am I going to know what to do? Jake always knew what to do. It is extremely scary being on your own for the first time in twenty-four years.

At least I know where he is. He is safe. Does that sound stupid?

I am now in isolation as Polly's husband believes he has Covid.

They helped me collect my shit from work a few days ago. I've got a work laptop but needed a few bits from the office.

It's okay though as I can still work and feel fine. Work's ramped up as no fucker can earn any money so my job (chasing people for money) is going swimmingly.

Me and Polly are already planning a huge session when this is all over with.

I keep thinking how Jake would be if he was here during this virus shit. I'd be sending him for supplies, cheesy puffs, Crunchies and diet cokes. All you need during a zombie apocalypse, I'm sure.

∗∗∗

Day one of home working. The prime minister is making an announcement later today, telling us the latest on the end of the fucking world.

It's quite scary but not as scary as being on my own without my protector.

It is majorly pissing me off hearing people moan that they can't see their loved ones because of lockdown. I know it's unfair but it feels so hurtful and selfish. I'd stay away from everyone if I could be locked down with Jake. Then I think how terrified I'd have been if Jake had made it through the operation as he'd likely be on kidney dialysis and be paralysed so he'd be incredibly vulnerable. Which he'd hate with a vengeance. He'd detest me fussing over him but I'd try to wrap him in bubble wrap.

Actually, I feel like I'm in a ridiculous bubble. I kind of am, I suppose, but I'm now the same as everyone else. Nobody can go anywhere and everybody is 'locked in'. It's strangely reassuring for me. Does that make sense?

I had an update from the coroners today. They said they have received the report on Jake's spinal cord today, which has now been forwarded to the pathologist along with the report on his heart for review.

The pathologist's final report giving the cause of death may take up to four weeks and they have said they will chase this up by the end of the month.

I cannot believe this is all still going on. It really doesn't seem real, and what with this ridiculous virus, my life feels very, very odd.

✳✳✳

Cannot get an online food shop for love nor money so I venture out to Waitrose.

There was a huge line outside the shop queuing down the road, hand sanitiser at the door with a 'bouncer' and a strict 'couple in, couple out' policy. Two metres apart and no lingering.

I was pretty good. I managed the essentials:

Baileys
Hula Hoops
Cheese
Orange Clubs

Sorted.

I have stuff in the freezer so I will be okay, I'm sure.

I crave Jake. I thought I felt him really lightly touch me in our bed tonight. I could also hear lots of creaking and the table in the front room looked like it was moving earlier.

I'm probably imagining it. Jake, please come home.

***

Oh, just fuck off.

First thing this morning, I decided to drop an entire water container onto the kitchen floor, as you do. Went everywhere. Then I cleaned it up and filled up the container, you know like one you put in the fridge to keep cold. I left it on the work surface while I did something else. It must've cracked when I dropped it on the floor so more water everywhere. Sometimes I am such a complete chump.

I still have the little water bottle Jake drank from the night before the operation. It is still in the fridge. It will probably still be there next year. It may carry botulism and would probably give Covid a run for its money.

∗∗∗

I knew today would be wank. I had a dream last night that Jake left me. It was hideous and I woke up in a shit mood and felt sad all day.

I have just opened a tin of beans for dinner and the ring pull snapped off.

FML.

∗∗∗

Today has been better.

Spoken to more people today than for the last three weeks. Maybe it is 'good to talk'.

If anyone asks, they get a stock response of 'I'm fine'.

FaceTime is the way forward. Imagine if you could FaceTime your loved ones up there! That would be epic.

I've started to collect white feathers. They're everywhere. My sister thinks that soon I can create my own white feathered Big Bird from *Sesame Street*.

I can barely see as I'm writing this. I'm clearly blind. I must wear my glasses more and stop winking whilst I type.

I worked for a couple of hours today even though it's Saturday as I pretty much failed on everything yesterday.

Had a video call with the Lollipops this evening and

consumed a few Baileys with them. We had a giggle.

Fish finger sandwich for dinner tonight. No judgment please and also sandwiches are not called sandwiches. They are called sammiches, okay? That's what Jake and me used to call them. He was a master sammich maker.

***

I am updating Jake on a daily basis about this Covid lark. Apparently, this lockdown may last for months. I told him he'd pull his hair out.

That then reminded me of his hair.

We were in Jersey a couple of Christmases ago on a mini break. We stayed in this beautiful centuries-old hotel, all low beams and roaring fires. The weather was shocking, but we persevered and walked around St Helier. It pissed down with rain so we stopped for a coffee in a little café. His hair was soaked right though and you could see his scalp through his hair, and I told him we should drop some cress seeds in there and we could grow some cress on his head.

He was thereon often referred to as cress head. I loved his cress head. He had it shorn to a grade two shortly afterwards to shut me up.

I seem to have developed a habit: online shopping. Better than coke, I suppose. I have just purchased a bright pink pea coat, faux leather biker jacket and two statement T-shirts. Mid-life crisis well and truly in force.

I ask Jake again whether he can see what is going on here with Covid. I'd love to know what he thinks. There is no one I'd rather be locked down with but I think he'd probably want to bash my head in by now.

It's annoying me that this is all I can talk to him about. Boring cow.

I ask him if he could come on by and talk to me but stipulate that he can't come at me all 'jaunty'. Do you know what I mean?

I'm a fan of all things supernatural. Jake was not. I am really unnerved by anything crawling on ceilings and walls or out of wells that walk or run in a jaunty manner.

Jake, please come back. That is all I want.

The Serious Investigation is delayed again due to Covid. I am not surprised. It isn't their fault. The hospitals are overrun with cases of Covid. It is quite horrifying.

I tell Jake I know he is looking down on me and checking I am okay. We always used to say he would not be going up (to heaven) but going down (to hell) as he was a bit of a fucker.

Funny how in real life this isn't so funny anymore.

I need to think more of our memories; I'm just babbling on about Covid and investigations and sodding coroners to him.

I love my husband so much.

April 2020

More memories: platters.

Our faves were traditional Italian or Spanish hams, cheeses and breads with olives and shit.

I have people round and knock up a platter, Indian: mini samosas, naan bread strips, tikka lamb, spicy prawns and all with dips and chutneys. Jake did a roast platter once. Sensational. Rare roast beef slices, chicken thighs, stuffing balls, roasted carrots, parsnips and roast potatoes with a jug of homemade gravy at the centre.

Oh, and hot platters full of breaded chicken, breads, mushrooms stuffed with gorgonzola and balsamic glaze.

We were at a pub with some of his siblings a few years ago. This pub wasn't a gastro delight, more of a pork scratchings kind of place but they did do basic food.

Jake looked at the menu (was pretty shite) and asked the manager if he could do a platter for us all. It was a legendary platter consisting of stuff likely to be at the back of the pub's freezer: mini sausages, chips, onion rings, chicken strips, garlic bread and, my personal favourite, roast parsnips. All served with bottles of barbeque sauce, ketchup and mayo.

Parsnips and mayo: don't knock it till you've tried it. Jake avoided this as he was too posh for parsnips!

Went down a treat after copious amounts of red wine. Most things do.

We went to Madeira in June of last year; it was our last holiday before his operation.

We pretty much had a platter every night. In Portugal and Madeira, it is the norm to be sitting in a bar and they will bring you a selection of snacks *for free*. It then temps you to look at the actual menu and then, before you know it, you have ordered half an Iberico pig and enough bread to soak up seventy-three litres of sangria.

This is why I will never be a size 12.

I wonder if Jake's cooking up a storm up there.

We went to Faro in 2018 for ten days. We had been to Portugal half a dozen times but this was the first time we stayed in Faro. Bloody brilliant. For two foodies, it was bliss.

We didn't stray too far the first night as we couldn't be arsed so we went to the nearest restaurant we could find. Jake had traditional peri-peri chicken and I had fish. It was lovely and we were pretty impressed.

The following days, the food just got better and better. Right up my cup of tea as Jake would've said.

The next night we went all out for a Mexican, not something we'd usually do as we like to stay traditional and eat what the locals eat whilst we're abroad. It was so good. We asked for it extra hot and I remember the waiter asking me if I was sure. I was. I was rewarded with a shot of tequila for finishing it without a sweat on. I am no quitter.

We went to a place that we named The Library. It was stunning inside. We ordered tapas. Greedy bastards. Jake was obsessed with what I think was loosely translated to stew pie. It was stunning. Fucking love pastry. We ordered seven dishes that night. They were mahoosive. We were on a tiny table and I shit you not, they brought over an overflow side table.

I could barely drink my wine I was so full. Barely.

Jake used to do loads of research wherever we went. He found a gorgeous restaurant called Pig and Cow. Highly recommend it. We went there a couple of times it was so good.

He also found a kind of sports bar that did this tubular calamari which we'd never seen before. So delicious.

Just remembered he also found a bar that sold red wine for €2. Rancid but did the trick and after three or four, no shits were given.

I also remember we walked miles on that holiday. Think that was one of the reasons we loved it so much as I had lost a bit of weight and kept up with him doing 20,000 steps plus a day just exploring.

Polly's coming round this evening.

We got wankered and FaceTimed our mum and dad last night. Sure they were so proud of their daughters.

I feel simply sparkling this morning. I feel gutted today. I keep crying. I miss him so much.

Things keep popping into my head. Not murderous thoughts or anything, just things that remind me of Jake.

He had to have his four front teeth replaced a few years back and had a titanium bridge fitted after he lost them in a falling down the stairs episode (sober).

He used to take them out in the evening if he was at home. It didn't bother me in the slightest. He looked handsome, teeth or no teeth.

He almost choked a couple of times when eating noodles. He used to call them 'conga noodles' as they used to conga down his throat as he couldn't cut them with his gums before they started to slide down the back of his throat. I obviously used to laugh in his face whilst he struggled not to choke to death. I was cruel. He soon learnt to pop the bridge back in if we ever had noodles.

He also used to say 'shut up' in this really teenage way if I pointed out something that he fucked up. It used to make me laugh so much.

Maybe you had to be there.

Anyway, that makes me laugh today. Deep breath, start again.

The family are still posting all things Covid related on our WhatsApp group. We're all checking in on one another. It is quite touching.

Apparently, our prime minister has got Covid and is in

hospital. Bollocks.

✷✷✷

I receive a package today via Ramazon (will explain later).

It's some tweezers. I thought I'd better start paying some attention to my chin hairs.

The packaging says 'Made in China' and I send a little video of this to Polly. She messages me back telling me to put the package down and back away!

Covid mania is afoot.

We had a little language we used to use. Now you may assume we were either ever so slightly simple or we were twelve. We were not.

Amazon – Ramazon (see)
Sandwich – sammich
Remote controls – montrols

Bless you – I can't spell this but Jake used to make this funny ERRHURRRHERRA noise every time I sneezed. He especially enjoyed doing this in public

The drift – my favourite duvet cover
Fancy a drink – paaarrrtttttty
Can I have a glass of water? – Vasa, bitch
Can I have some dessert please? – Pudding, bitch
See you shortly – Don't call me shorty

> Central heating for grown-ups – wine
> Educate – edumacate
> Better – betterer
> Dirty Bastard – anyone foreign
> Salad – ralad

I have no idea why we did this, we just did. Still makes me smile.

I remember when we went to Grenada and Barbados for our ten-year wedding anniversary. It was a beautiful holiday, but my favourite memory is the both of us watching a steel band play in this jungle-like outside area. Jake went up to the bar to get us a drink; we were sitting on a big semi-circle plush settee big enough for twelve people.

I watched Jake walk back from the bar with our drinks. I could see him walking up to the back of the settee in front of ours. I realised there was another blonde with similar hair to me (plus he was half cut) and he was kind of bending down to whisper in her ear. I shouted his name and luckily it was loud enough over the thrum of the steel drums for him to turn around and see me.

He staggered back, no fucks were given and he was pissing himself, especially as the chap next to her was large. I would have been mortified but he thought it was hilarious.

Good times.

I am trying so hard to think only of all the wonderful memories I have of us.

I am not sure if it is helping as it is so painful thinking I'll never walk off a plane with him into a new country and smile at each other knowing we are going to have a new adventure together.

That makes me remember when we went to the Dominican Republic about fifteen years ago. I was sunbathing and Jake was bored and said he was going off to explore.

I left him to it. I turned onto my tummy and looked up and saw he had walked up to two armed guards at the entrance to the beach and was chatting to them. I closed my eyes and I knew he would be okay.

Two hours later, he wandered out of the fucking jungle in a pool of sweat looking as pleased as punch.

He then proceeded to tell me he had to sign some kind of disclaimer for those guards as he wanted to go to an area they wouldn't recommend for tourists as it was quite dangerous. Not people-wise, just wildlife etc. He claims he saw a snake. Reckon it was a small snake. He loved an adventure.

I do not like putting past tense when I'm speaking about him.

***

It's Easter weekend. Jake always spoilt me at Easter. We used to do the Daily Mail Easter egg hunt; I think I enjoyed it more than he did.

I cannot bring myself to go out and buy the paper though, plus it's diseased out there in the real world and may be full of zombies.

I loved our life so much.

I ask Jake to do something today so I knew he's with me at home.

I was doing the washing up at the time. The sun was shining through the back door. I looked to my left and saw hundreds and hundreds of tiny washing up bubbles. It was almost ethereal. They were coming down and landing on just me.

I one hundred percent think Jake was telling me he was with me.

✳✳✳

Easter Sunday today.

Video call with the sisters-in-law and Patricia was fellating a black dildo. Ask no questions.

Had FaceTime with the Lollipops this evening and was really nice seeing them.

Greg's coming over (socially distanced, obviously) tomorrow to look at my front garden. That isn't a euphuism. It really does need sorting. Jake was the gardener, not me. In fact, Jake was the doer of everything. I was a lazy bitch.

Cuba memories.

We went on honeymoon to Varadero. It was my first trip abroad.

It was cancelled just before we went as some hurricane had destroyed the area in Cuba that we were originally going to but we changed to a part which wasn't affected.

I was crapping myself about going abroad. It wasn't something I was really into. Mum and Dad never went anywhere and therefore we didn't go anywhere as kids.

I remember the feeling of stepping off the plane and thinking that the heat was coming from the aeroplane, but it wasn't. It was roasting.

There were teeny weeny little frogs all along a walkway to the hotel lobby.

Jake suffered from prickly heat. Such a Brit abroad. I remember sitting on the beach rubbing sun tan lotion on his back and cringing as it was like rubbing it into The Thing from *The Fantastic Four*. I don't think he was impressed at my analogy.

We went out for dinner one evening away from the resort. Jake had picked out this restaurant whilst wandering about (his favourite thing to do) and I was probably sunning myself on a lounger somewhere.

This outside restaurant took 'al fresco' to a whole new level. It was full of locals so we knew it'd be good. I had 'fruit de la mer' and it was sensational.

The owner of the place looked like Danny DeVito, couldn't speak a word of English but was so friendly. I asked him where the loos were and he took me. He obviously understood 'toilets' in a Spanish accent. They were scary, a dark cabin full of insects. My worst nightmare. But, for some reason, it was okay, partly down to some wine but mostly down to the wonderful atmosphere and just being in a different part of the world.

Danny DeVito flagged us down a taxi to go back to the hotel and for some reason, we had a partial police escort down the Varadero strip, looking out of the taxi window watching a storm starting to form over the sea. Bloody amazing night.

When we were away, he used to like to swim in the pool or the sea in a kind of sideways motion and sidle up to me and pretend to be Pepe Le Pew in a mock French accent — that cartoon skunk. God, that used to make me die. If you don't remember Pepe, look him up.

We went a year or so later to Guardalavaca. That was Jake's favourite destination. It was truly stunning, proper paradise. But it had spiders, big fucking spiders.

Jake thought it would be hilarious to get down on his knees and have a little chat with this monstrous tarantula that had ventured into the hotel foyer. Jesus, I lost my shit that night.

I also recall walking into the gents by accident and being accosted by some iffy Russian dude. Serves me right.

Visiting Cuba with Jake meant we learnt so much about the Cuban culture and it really did humble us.

One of our favourite moments was sitting by this old ramshackle hut which was right on this picture-perfect white and turquoise beach, drinking rum punch and Cuba Libres whilst an old Cuban vagrant in a scruffy torn Thomas Cook T-shirt was chatting to us and asking us for Pesos. He got a few.

Jake taught me how to swim under a little bridge in the pool whilst holding my breath. I was like an eight-year-old.

We went to a bat cave and I was in my element like Dora the Explorer. Jake was so impressed with me. Bats are not spiders though.

I am off on one now. Memories flooding to the forefront of my mind.

I remember our wedding day like it was yesterday.

I'm not sure if I ever thought we'd get married, for no other reason than we were so happy. But I do think our lives got better once we got married. It's not for everyone and to be fair, I was Jake's third wife but it cemented us.

I chose to have just one bridesmaid for the wedding: my eighteen-month-old niece.

A couple of days prior to the big day, she went to hospital with suspected meningitis. It was a scary couple of days but she was okay. When I look back at the wedding photos, she looks so pale!

I got my 'hair did' and it actually looked phenomenal thanks to my fabulous hairdresser who I still use to this day, even when applying my make-up, it went right. This rarely happens to me.

The weather was okay even though it was not the

summer. I turned up and, in true Jake style, I was reliably informed (his mates grassed him up) that he had only just turned up. He may or may not have gone for a swift couple of pints. Prick.

He told me I looked beautiful and, on that day, I really did feel it. I buggered up my vows but it just added to the happiness of that day.

One day, I will watch our wedding video again, but not at the moment. I don't think I could handle it.

The reception was epic. The food was out of this world and we had a free bar — obviously.

I remember coming home after the wedding with bags of presents and cards; we were half cut (I know, right).

We went through all the packages and envelopes and we were overwhelmed by everyone's generosity. Unfortunately, in the morning, we realised that, although we were so pleased to receive all of the gifts and cash, we had absolutely no fucking idea who had given us what as I had just ripped through all the gifts like a woman possessed.

I am so incredibly proud to be your wife, Jake.

The memories just keep on coming. I don't know if it's helping me or making me even more devastated!

We were invited to a 'soiree' last August with all of Jake's family. I'm looking at the photos now. He looks so happy. One of his sisters said he didn't look well but I thought that was shite. I don't understand how just four months later, I lost him.

We knew at this stage that he would have to have an operation.

When we took the pics, instead of 'say cheese', I said 'everyone say aneurysm'. Not so funny now.

I also have just thought of our 'tequila related booking'.

Jesus, it was my dad's seventieth and we went on a boat trip. Me and my sister argued as we had a few glasses of vino and Jake wasn't feeling all that great (this was the first time Jake had started to get unwell and this was 2015). We left after a few hours and went back home. I was really upset for arguing with my sister so to remedy this, Jake opened a bottle of pomegranate tequila. Why not, we had just come back from Mexico.

Are you thinking what jammy fuckers we were? Trust me, we knew it. We really did make the most of all our holidays. We lived for them.

Anyway, we sat in our garden drinking said tequila and Jake's brother and new wife were at Gatwick Airport waiting to fly out to Portugal for their honeymoon. We FaceTimed them. Doom.

They asked us to come and stay at the villa they had hired. Now, bear in mind, we had literally been back from Mexico for about a week.

The next thing I recall was Jake coming into the bedroom the next morning whilst I was feeling extremely sorry for myself and showing me his emails. Yes. We had booked a flight to fucking Portugal for three days' time.

The car journey with my then boss the following Monday was interesting. Luckily, he had a sense of humour and in my leaving speech a year or so later, he referred to it as the 'tequila related booking'.

✳✳✳

I boiled an egg this morning. When I say boiled, I mean dry cooked. For thirty-five minutes. I cannot be trusted.

I have just thought of something that happened years and years ago. I'm not sure how to put this into words!

You may have gathered by now that Jake had a reputation of being a bit of a flirt. When we first got together, his pals were always winding me up about his ex-girlfriend. I had never met her but my twenty-four-year-old brain had built her up to be my arch nemesis.

They told me she looked like Elle Macpherson. This was not good. I do not look like a supermodel. The more they told me this, the more paranoid I got. I was only in my early twenties and not confident one little bit.

This particular evening, the lads were persistent in the ruse to wind me up and I bit. They even asked the barman at our then local to confirm what she looked like and I was furious.

Jake had booked us a hotel that night and it was really plush. I distinctly recall that, upon entering the hotel, the TV screen said, 'welcome Mr and Mrs Forrester'. I bloody loved that.

I was like a woman possessed and we had the most intense session that evening and I said, whilst sucking on Jake's balls, 'I bet Elle Mac fucking pherson didn't do that.' For fuck's sake.

Anyway, evidently, she didn't and a good time was had by all.

I found out a few days later that:

> A. They paid the barman to say that his ex looked like Elle
> B. She didn't look like Elle

I also remember: space soup.

On another one of our holidays, we went to the Dominican Republic. It was amazing and for our anniversary, Jake had arranged for us to have dinner on the beach.

The hotel staff set it up and it was beautiful. However, it was a tad breezy. The waiter kept trying to light these huge fire torches which blew out pretty much each time he lit them. He eventually poured some fuel onto them to keep them alight.

Our first course was soup. I have never laughed so much in my life. This bloody lobster bisque was blowing as if we were in space with all these bubbles floating from the spoon and we were trying to catch the soup bubbles.

Happy, happy days.

***

These memories just keep on coming. Sodding Facebook is killing me.

We went to NYC for Jake's birthday last year.

It was my fave trip. Have I said that about all of them?

So many things happened but one memory that sticks out, as it was 'so Jake', was that as we left JFK airport, he wanted to have a ciggie. So, we quickly checked where to get a cab from and it all looked relatively easy so off he went and had a cigarette whilst I babysat the cases.

Once he'd finished his cigarette, we walked round the corner and realised that the queue to what we thought was for the taxis into the city was actually just the end of this enormously long queue which began in the airport itself.

Now Jake was not known for his patience. In fact, he could be very rude and would push himself through queues as he didn't like to hang about. He caught a turbaned yellow cab driver's eye and the bloke called to us from the middle of the queue and told us to get in.

Other taxi drivers were doing their nut as we had jumped the queue and the taxi driver just shouted to them, 'crazy motherfuckers' and then started his engine and said, 'Welcome to NYC, folks.' I swear if we had not got in that cab, it would've taken us at least an hour before we could get in a cab.

I treasure those five days.

✳✳✳

One of Jake's sisters sent me a random message today advising that I should hear some news today.

No idea what she was on about so messaged her to say so. She was chasing up the results from the coroners.

I tell her I spoke with the coroners last week who are still chasing this report and they said they would call me as soon as they have it.

Some people can't seem to comprehend that I don't relish knowing what happened. Why would I? Would it bring him back? They want justice. I just want my husband back.

Later today, I get the results back after they call me. They explain in detail and send me a full explanation.

I can't take it in. I don't tell anyone but Polly.

Jake had chronic heart disease, so all of the previous symptoms he went to the doctors for, the high BP, chest pains, swollen legs, congestion, fainting and dizziness and being knackered, were probably to do with this. Shouldn't this have been diagnosed before he went in for an operation of this magnitude?

Does this mean he could have had surgery to correct this and that he could have lived? Could he have been treated before he had the fucking operation and if so, maybe that could've saved him?

This was my fear. The fear that I had not done enough

to make sure he lived through this.

Could I have saved him, should I have done more?

I cannot tell his family yet. This is what they believed all along but I didn't.

∗∗∗

Polly is coming round tonight. Due to Covid lockdown we can't go to the pub so we're having a pub night here instead.

I've made a bar at the dining room table. You have to have an imagination in these times.

∗∗∗

I am so tired; we went for it last night.

Polly chucked a glass of Prosecco over Jake's new home (the box his ashes are in). She feels awful but I said he would have wanted to join in and have a drink for sure.

∗∗∗

I have finally plucked up the courage and told his family about the coroner's report.

I let them know that, as I understand it, Jake already had heart disease. This caused his heart to fail and consequently caused an inadequate blood supply to his spinal cord, which is why they believe he became paralysed during the operation.

The coroners say, due to the implications involved, it is

likely that this will go to an inquest.

I have requested all of his medical records from his doctor today as in my opinion based on the report (although this hasn't yet been confirmed) that despite all the tests he had since 2015 when he began to first feel unwell, they didn't diagnose heart disease. I am a mess.

I tell his family I don't have the answers and I am just trying to take it all in so I can't help them understand. I have not told his kids yet. I can't.

It is extremely painful to think his death may have been avoided if this had been detected.

If this is correct and it was a case of misdiagnosis, I will not take it lying down. I can't. I need to fight for Jake. It's not for financial gain but I have lost the love of my life and his family have lost their brother and father.

The lead investigator for the SI team contacts me reference the ongoing separate investigation via the trust. She has asked for Jake's files to be sent directly to me and suggests that when I get them, I do not read them on my own. The contents are likely to be disturbing.

Apparently, the investigation is their top priority and she is pushing hard to get the panel together to review the case.

Covid is obviously not helping matters, but I understand.

In my heart of hearts, I don't (or can't) think that any of the doctors or surgeons are at fault but possibly his GP for not diagnosing the heart disease. He has been for many tests since 2015 since he was unwell after coming back from Mexico. He had a hiatus hernia which he was told was not big enough for an op to fix it. He had numerous tubes and cameras into his stomach and lastly, he was diagnosed with high blood pressure in 2018. It came from nowhere. He'd never had high blood pressure then all of a sudden, he began to feel under the weather and as they do, they checked his BP and it was dangerously high.

He had been back and forth to the GP and had even been to hospital for further tests to try to control the BP. The side effects he got from numerous different BP medications were horrendous. Tinnitus, insomnia, lethargy, nausea and chest pains. He even had pains in his legs and they were concerned he had a DVT but it ended up he pulled a muscle probably by pushing himself so much. You put all of this together and it seems obvious it was his heart.

The thing is, with Jake, in the twenty-four years I was with him, he didn't go to the doctors for anything until 2015. He shook off all sorts of bugs and shit. He never complained and was a fan of 'just getting on with it' whereas I'm more of a fan of 'dramatising the shit out of any ailment I may have'.

So, when he genuinely couldn't shake off feeling crap, he went to the doctors.

I tell Jake I am handling this shit. I realise I am stronger than I give myself credit for.

Jake always told me I was strong. I should have trusted him on that.

My head is banging.

I think I should try to concentrate on some happier memories as I'm finding it increasingly difficult to deal with life in general.

✳✳✳

Covid is shit, but I am working from home, which I really like. Being home means feeling close to Jake.

Everyone is in lockdown and for me this is okay. We're all in the same boat. What happens when everything returns to 'normal'? I don't think there is a normal for me.

I met up with a friend back last summer and we had a blast day drinking in Winchester. I'd arranged to meet up with Jake in Woking in the evening and I called him once I got to the station as I was a little worse for wear (are you realising that I am a complete drunken lush yet?).

He walked up to the station to collect me and we were on the phone the whole time he was walking towards the station. He got to where I was supposed to be but couldn't see me.

He asked me if I could see any landmarks. I could. I was not in Woking. I was in fucking Basingstoke.

He told me to get my arse back on a train to Woking and then he would meet me in a nice bar in town. I managed it. I was so grateful to see him when I finally got off at the correct stop that I had completely sobered up.

Four months later, I met up with Polly for a pre-Christmas drink. I messaged him to say that we had decided that me and her were going to Prague together in the New Year.

He messaged me back to say: 'You got lost coming back from fucking Winchester'.

Wise words, Jake, wise words.

May 2020

How is it May already?

I am so thankful I am working from home. It allows me my own bubble of 'normality'.

This Covid debacle's 'getting real' but it doesn't scare me, apart from the thought of my family and friends being affected in any way.

I've been going through the worst thing I could imagine already so a global pandemic doesn't faze me.

I like being locked away, locked away in my own bubble of fucking doom.

I miss you, Jake, so much, I was looking at some pictures earlier and my heart quivered at the sight of his face. I get now that Jake is still my protector.

I had some tarot cards done by a friend's daughter. I sent her my picture and she said she would do me a reading virtually. She knew nothing of my circumstances and I trusted my friend not to have tipped her off.

The reading was incredible. She read my cards and said:

> *I picked up a strong male presence and asked him for a card. He has shown me the King of Wands which is a card of protection. He has shown me that he wants you*

to let go of something that is imprisoning you and you must do this in order to move on.

But his protection is around you always. He is a charismatic and strong presence and made himself known. I also have the Empress card which represents harmony and security in your future and he again oversees this with you. The Wheel card emphasises that you will start to look at things in your life more positively and this will transform your way of thinking with a newfound confidence. I have another male that comes through that is not of the spirit world but is present in your lift who is honest and loyal.

Wow. This made me cry but in a happy way. I wish I could see him but he does visit my BFF Charley. She's a 'sensitive'. I tell Jake that if he comes through to me, I won't be scared but I understand now that he doesn't want to scare me.

The guilt she refers to could be so many things.

I feel guilty I let him have the operation. I feel so guilty that I didn't hold him for longer the morning he left to have the op. I feel guilty that I was pissed off that I may have to try to make the trip to the hospital to visit him over Christmas. I feel guilty I am not closer to his kids. I feel guilty I haven't pressed as hard to conclude the investigation. I feel guilty that I snorted a whole load of coke on the day of the funeral.

I feel guilty for everything.

I start watching stuff that Jake used to like that I didn't get into.

Peaky Blinders. Why didn't I watch this? It's epic.

Boris is letting us know on Sunday whether lockdown is being relaxed. It is crazy. Jake seriously would have flouted the rules one hundred percent.

✳✳✳

Happy VE Day, Jake!

I keep finding shit to do to keep my mind occupied. So far I've:

- Cleaned the carpet on my hands and knees with carpet cleaner
- Swapped my winter wardrobe for my spring/ summer wardrobe
- Vacuum-packed shit loads of Jake's clothes
- Cut down the insanely large bush in my front garden
- Housework
- Made chicken nuggets for this evening: the dish of kings
- Made a bolognese for the freezer

I was supposed to call Cora this evening but I slacked her off as she does my nut in. Full of doom and gloom and judgy as fuck.

I hate bank holidays now. I know that Jake and I would've definitely been drunk by now. We loved an extended weekend.

I cannot stop doing shit. It makes me realise what a lazy bitch I was. Jake did everything around the house.

I have swept the leaves in the back garden, pulled out some weeds and watered the garden.

My work have sent me a rose plant and written a lovely note just saying they're thinking about me.

I have a FaceTime call this evening with the Lollipops; we have decided to 'dress up'.

I wear a vest top and jeggings but accessorise with sparkly cat ears and drawn-on freckles. No idea. I think I am trying to channel a Snapchat filter.

If anyone comes to the door, I'm fucked.

I have a pre-party drink of vodka and tonic. The fact I'm excited by a bloody video call goes to show how dire the current situation is.

I am having a cigarette outside and my neighbour shouts out to me so I go over and have a quick chat with her, completely forgot I'm wearing cat ears and drawn-on freckles.

She is as deaf as a post so maybe she's blind too as she seems completely unaware of my get up.

***

Oh dear. The highlight of today was finding a 'life hack' for folding my box of Weetabix into a little house. Ridiculous. I have done it on all my boxes of cereal.

I have not stopped eating today. I think I may have worms.

Boris is announcing to the country what is the next step for lockdown later today.

Watch this space.

I had a random call from an old friend last night.

I knew him when I was about seventeen and haven't seen him for twenty-five years plus. He got my number from Greg. I was a bit tipsy when he called, otherwise I would have ignored his call. He was pleasant enough but he implied that he had always fancied me and it made me feel a bit 'ick' talking to another man in Jake's house. I reassured Jake that it would not happen again!

***

Today, I have made my first curry. It's currently simmering away. I used chicken thighs as a homage to Jake. Would never normally use thighs as I am a breast girl and it used to drive him nuts that he had to de-fat and de-vein all meat so I could just eat nice fluffy (?) chicken, steak or any other meat.

I winged cooking it completely and used a shit load of spices that I think Jake would use!

Am I the only person who feels proper 'chefy' when

you put water in the empty tinned tomato can and give it a shake to use all the juice up?

✳✳✳

I went into the office today. It was quite nice to see a few people.

The MD told me I looked thin. Literally the only advantage of Jake not feeding me his superior meals.

I ate the curry. It was fucking hot and my mouth was burning. Jake would have liked it.

I thought of a few things today that made me smile.

When Jake first had his aneurysm diagnosis, he took it upon himself to not only give up smoking but also to get as fit as he could. He met me one lunchtime in the park near my office and rocked up in jeans, a shirt and normal trainers. I remember watching him jog back. It was hilarious and he looked ridiculous but cute. He also ran up and down the grotty old stairs in a car park near us until he got out of breath. I remember reading in the local online news that there was a report of a pervert hanging around there. Obviously, I suggested this could have been him wheezing and sweating.

I remember on one of our holidays before we flew to wherever we were going that we stayed in a hotel in the airport. We'd checked in our luggage the previous evening and only had hand luggage to take with us. He packed a new shirt that he hadn't worn before to wear on the flight.

I hadn't seen him in it and I was walking behind him in the hotel foyer ready to check out. He turned around to say something to me and I literally collapsed. The shirt was so tight it could barely do up round his little tummy. He was not impressed. We bought him a new shirt at the airport so he wouldn't suffocate.

We used to have a cat called Muffin. I got really peed off with her one day as she had destroyed something with her murderous claws and told her I was going to give her away. I got home from work and she sauntered passed me with a tiny homemade knapsack tied to her back.

I asked Jake what was going on. He said, 'She's leaving.' God, he made me laugh constantly.

He used to pack me little surprise snacks every time we went away. I would open my suitcase and find an array of my favourite snacks. He made me an Easter cake once, melted chocolate with more chocolate. Once again hindering any possibility of my endless weight loss goals. I loved it really. He also used to put carrots with most 'normal' meals for colour.

He made a retro buffet once for a party and did curried eggs and they went down a treat. At the same party, he also got a colleague of mine so drunk (male and in his sixties) that he was eating jalapenos out of a jar by the dozen. Another colleague of mine was also extremely drunk and to cure his drunkenness, Jake fed him pineapple chunks off of the retro cheese and pineapple sticks.

People called him Floyd after Keith Floyd. Our parties were legendary.

When we went to NYC, I made him walk across Brooklyn Bridge. It was freezing and he got chapped lips. He did not let me forget that.

He used to buy my mum loads of veg from the market every time she came over, just because he was quite literally the perfect son-in-law and would milk it at every opportunity. He also said that cauliflower counted as flowers for her. I am so lucky to have been married to him. I miss him so very much

***

Got the skin and blister over this evening.

As we are not able to go anywhere because of Covid, I am setting up the dining room table again as a little bar. It feels like a wine night.

I put on a top I bought online a couple of years ago, I remember browsing on my phone lying on a sunbed whilst on holiday and ordering it. It has never fitted me as it was way too tight. It actually fits.

The 'heartbreak diet' may finally be working! Have to take the positives.

***

This world can really be an utter cunt.

Polly and me were having a lovely time last night. I actually felt okay and kind of happy for the first time in months. I got a text from a friend of mine. She told me that another very good friend of mine's husband died on Friday.

I am heartbroken for her. She has a young daughter who's only two or three.

Why? *Why?* It makes me so, so sad. Selfishly, it's almost as though, just as I start to be able to control how I feel, something gets thrown into the mix to fuck it up.

I can feel her pain and it breaks my already broken heart.

I speak to Jake and ask him to look after her husband, telling him that he was an avid Brexiter so they should get on very well.

I am so tired today and I am having a shit day. I just can't help thinking of my friend and it brings it all back to me.

Every day I think of Jake and every single day I miss him. Every day I wish he was at my side.

✳✳✳

The inquest into Jake's death begins today, almost six months since it happened.

His family think it is no coincidence that his father passed away on today's date twenty-six years ago!

I don't feel too bad considering. It has been such a long time coming that maybe it is better to be concluding. What with Covid and everything, it all feels so very unreal.

I have received all of Jake's medical records from the

hospital. I cannot read them yet. I am honestly too scared to go through them. The files they have sent are enormous. I also have ten or twelve online files to go through that the hospital have sent via email.

This week has been horrendous. My next door neighbour tried to top herself yesterday.

Yesterday morning, I saw a paramedic van outside the house and it made my stomach turn. I could hear them knocking but I couldn't make out if it was definitely next door.

My doorbell then went and a paramedic asked if I had a key to next door (I don't) and if he could access her place from the back via my garden. Obviously, I let him in. He shimmied over the fence and I could hear him shouting her name. Luckily, she had left a window open so he could get in.

I couldn't watch so I went back inside and tried to do some work, but they knocked again and I could see them wheeling her into the back of the van. She was unconscious and her mouth was open and eyes were shut. She is over seventy and lives on her own.

He gave me her keys and said she's got cats. I said I'll sort it. He told me I could call the hospital later to see how she's doing.

I was at a loss of what to do. I didn't feel I had the capacity to look after somebody else.

Thankfully, her son and daughter-in-law turned up later that day and I explained that whilst I was happy to feed the cats, I was not able to do anything else and told them my circumstances asking them to keep me up-to-date.

They took the key and said they would be able to sort it anyway.

I know it sounds selfish but I'm relieved I don't have to go into her empty house or call the hospital. I am not sure if I could deal with it.

I sat in my garden after they left. Tears were pouring from my eyes.

I have a little pathway next to my garden that leads to our back gate. I can almost hear Jake walking down the path with a bag of food shopping. The feeling I have that if I reached out, I would touch him feels almost tangible.

He used to like using the back gate when I was in the shower, knock on the outside of the bathroom window and scare the shit out of me.

The garden backs onto the railway tracks. The train line isn't a busy one, maybe four an hour. I am so scared to look at the trains as I think that maybe Jake is on one of the trains and I might not be able to get to him. What would I do? Run after the train?

I urgently need to get my head in a better place.

I need to remember the good times but without the thought of never doing them again with him.

Think. Think of good things. Here it goes.

Quarteira.

One of our favourite holiday destinations in the Algarve but a quieter little town right opposite the beach.

We had a dirty little secret out there. A bar called Fantasia. Rough as you like, full of Brits and they served roast dinners and you could smoke at the bar, hence why Jake loved it so much. Also had their own bookie that took your bets whilst you watched racing. Fucking awful but he loved it. I loved the fact I could have a double Tia Maria and coke for €2 and they played a lot of Abba. We had an apartment almost on top of the bar one year and they used to make us a jug of sangria to take upstairs each evening.

We also found a lovely little restaurant called Mirobriga. The owner was a woman who seemed to love flirting with Jake, but she was really nice. They used to serve cold carrots in olive oil. WTF? Apparently, it was a Portuguese delicacy and used be served as a *couvert*... kind of like a pre-starter starter. We ate it as we liked to be as close to local as possible. They were pretty rank but the rest of the food was stunning.

I'll go back there again one day as I know Jake would like that.

***

I have put some fairy lights up in my garden today. Looks pretty.

Had a 'three-way' with the girls today. By three-way, of course, I mean a video call.

We had a theme: The Adams Family. I was Wednesday. We all looked ridiculous and I drank a bottle of white wine.

White wine gives me heartburn and makes me angry. Great choice. I felt okay though. Revelation.

Then watched a bit of *Pretty Woman* and ate chocolate.

✳✳✳

Greg and Natalie pop round for a social distanced afternoon in the garden.

I did not intend on drinking and had lined up a couple of iced coffees as it's really hot, but Greg brought round some Stellas and I ended up drinking a pint of Baileys.

It is a bank holiday.

They keep checking on me asking how I am.

'I'm fine,' I say.

I am getting drunk on a constant basis. Maybe it is good for me but maybe it's not. I don't know. Sometimes when I'm drinking, I feel better but the next day, I usually feel like shit. Not in a hungover way but in a depressed way.

I should really know better by now but I like the way it makes me feel at the time.

✳✳✳

I'm sober today. It's Bank Holiday Monday. I hate bank holidays. They seem endless.

I sleep for a while then binge watch another serial killer documentary.

I'll get over myself tomorrow.

∗∗∗

Sometimes I look around and I see his face. I'm looking at him right now in a photo and he's wearing a short sleeved white shirt with red chilli peppers on it and he's holding a glass of red wine. The picture was taken in a restaurant in Faro and he's so happy.

My cushion is behind me and in that picture, he's holding a vape and looking less than impressed and pulling a face.

Sometimes, when I am in the front room lying on the floor trying to do some kind of exercise (I know, right), I can see his face in the spotlights in our hallway. I have told my sister about this and she has lain down in the same place but can't see what I think I can see.

When I go to bed at night, I make 'a Jake' to lie next to me. I place his dressing gown and the cushion I have with his face on it on the pillow next to me. I need to feel him next to me.

I see his photos on the wall on his side of the bed and he looks so bloody gorgeous it makes me smile then cry.

I miss him so much. The emptiness just won't go away but then I don't think I want it to go away.

∗∗∗

I have a video call with the Lollipops this evening. Except one Lollipop is going rogue and breaking lockdown rules and is coming over and staying as a house guest! Sometimes rules need to be broken.

Our theme is pink, obviously.

We intend to drink wine and eat pizza and sing Motown.

Lola and I thought it would be a brilliant idea to make a homemade ouija board whilst being a little bit drunk and try to contact Jake.

I really don't know why I do these things to myself.

Of course, Jake came through and told me that I needed to 'LIVE'.

There was a lot that he said that Lola would not have been aware of: dates of things etc.

Therefore, I am going with it.

We lit a candle. A fucking red one? It should have been white as per paranormal research protocol. The wax from this candle is also all over my pale grey carpet.

Googled how to get rid of the wax. You put ice cubes in a tea towel and iron through it, which works in case you're interested.

Oh, and one of the hob rings turned on or I accidently turned it on whilst drunk.

I know what I believe.

June 2020

How can it be almost six months since he went?

I am not looking forward to this week as it is my birthday but Jake promised me, through my ouija board session, that he will do something. I'll be raging if he doesn't.

I have just ordered an actual ouija board from Ramazon. Who knew the kind of shit you can get from Ramazon.

I want to be able to speak to him again; like my own personal Nokia to Jake's new world.

Had a cry this morning. Feeling very low. Need to keep my chin up.

I get tired of people telling me how well I am doing, but I'm not. I keep it hidden.

I will live though. I promised him I would, so I cannot let him down.

I am fine.

***

Charley and her daughter Louise (my goddaughter) come over today — again breaking lockdown rules — but my friends can see I am struggling.

Guess what we do?

The ouija board again. This time it is done properly. Charley is what you would call a 'sensitive'. She knows her shit.

She does a protection prayer for us and we begin. Obviously, I couldn't give two shits about speaking to anyone else. I only want to speak to Jake.

We ask the obligatory questions, then get a little more specific so I can be sure it really is Jake.

We ask for the date of our wedding, and the initials of the singer of our first dance song and ask him to spell out something she wouldn't know.

He tells us the date of our wedding, and goes to 'OR' for the initials — Charley wouldn't know that as, although she's my best friend, she wouldn't remember that actual date nor our wedding dance as it's quite obscure.

We ask him to spell out something that only I would know. He goes to the letter J.

We have taped the session and listen to it afterwards.

There's nothing much until he goes to the letter J. He *says* 'middle name' in a voice just like his. He has two middle names and one begins with P and the other J; the second middle name only his family would know as he doesn't use it.

It's Joseph and I'm shocked. I keep rewinding it and listening to it.

By the time the girls go, I feel physically drained. I

think that connecting with Jake has put me through the wringer but in a wonderful way. I couldn't ask for a better pre-birthday gift.

***

My Birthday

I feel so emotional today. I can't stop the tears. I thought I'd be okay but I'm not.

Fuck it. I post a shit load of photos plus I write this on Facebook:

> *I wasn't going to do this as I find it so hard looking back at our memories but as it's my birthday, a day I just wanted to forget, I wanted to make it about Jake 🖤 Every one of those pics was in a different country and on my birthday. This is the first birthday I've spent here for years! Until you lose someone, you don't realise quite how utterly wonderful they are. He spoilt me rotten on my birthday and I know I'm lucky to have had him in my life for so many years. Not a day goes past where I don't miss him. I talk to him constantly and he is still the most important person in my life and will always be my No. 1. I'm so lucky to have amazing people in my life who have supported me. Thank you all, you know who you are. So, happy fucking birthday to me. My sister and*

me will be drinking through this and I've been reliably informed that Jake's already on the vino 🖤 🖤 *Cheers.*

I never thought I'd be one of those pilchards who posts stuff about their life on Facebook but I enjoy sharing my thoughts with my friends. They can always scroll passed if they don't like it, I suppose.

Polly and me get hammered. We dance to eighties classics and drink way too much wine and vodka. We randomly Facetime with an old friend and her husband.

Bed beckons at 3 a.m. Regrets are going to be strong tomorrow.

I just want this day over with.

The thing with Facebook is, as handy as it can be, it can also be an absolute arse ache. For instance, today, I woke up to a shit load of Facebook memories of me and Jake on our holidays.

Now, not only does this make me realise we were right pain in the arses parading our holiday pics to all and sundry but also if you're not in the best place, it can really take you down.

I reassure myself that I should be thankful that we were always on holiday as this year it definitely wouldn't be happening due to the travel ban with Covid.

To be honest with you, I wouldn't be wanting to go anywhere this year regardless of this virus. Maybe it has done me a favour. It's like a surreal dream or nightmare.

✳✳✳

My friend Cora's husband is really not very well. She is saying the doctors are ninety-five percent sure he has cancer. I ask Jake to send him a message to keep fighting. I am so scared for her, but I don't know what I can offer her. I am trying to be supportive but realistically, and also selfishly, I just want to curl up and ignore her calls.

Looks like the pub gardens may be opening in a couple of weeks. I hope so.

Yesterday was a funny day. Not funny ha ha, just odd. It felt kind of flat.

I wish I could feel happy, Jake. I just find it so hard without you.

My neighbour is on the mend. Thank God. She is coming home soon. I got a nice message from her son updating me.

I went into work today and it was okay. I am so glad I am able to work. It really has been a godsend.

Made a little visit to Sainsbury's for essentials: wine, crisps and cheese.

My sisters-in-law have said they'll come over in a couple of weeks for a social distanced garden party. Said we'd do it for Polly as her birthday is coming up at the end of this month.

It's exactly six months since you went. How is this possible?

I console myself by watching a whole load of *90 Day Fiancé* episodes.

I post something on Facebook to mark the day. It says:

> *Marry a man who says things like:*
> *You are beautiful*
> *I am proud of you*
> *You can do anything*
> *No, four glasses of wine isn't a lot*
> *I married that man. I miss that man.*
> *I'll be with him again one day.*

✳✳✳

Went to Mum and Dad's for a BBQ today. My brother-in-law is trying to outdo the prodigal perfect son-in-law (Jake) and cooked for us.

It wasn't a patch on Jake's efforts but God loves a tryer.

I am now getting myself ready for a video call with the Lollipops. Our theme is the Oscars.

I have purchased some gold face paint and a sparkly sequinned gold top from good old Ramazon. I have painted my face gold, added several gold accessories (a la B. A. Baracus), and have gone as an Oscar. The things you do to pass the time. I look a state.

✳✳✳

I haven't cried this week so far. Not even this morning when I woke up with a hangover and full of regret. My vodka game was strong last night. I blame the Lollipops. I also know I made a couple of unauthorised calls to some people, probably talking utter shit but I needed to talk.

I am sure Jake would be proud of my antics.

I am now ready for the day. The telly is lined up with shit reality TV and I am fully carb loaded.

Life is not as good as it was with Jake, but dare I say it's getting slightly better than it was a month or two ago. I actually don't know how I coped a few months ago.

Got a gutty feeling today. Trying to keep myself busy to push it away.

I have received more medical records from the hospital today.

There is stuff in there referring to chronic kidney disease. Did Jake tell me everything?

I'm just not ready to read them all yet. I need to wait until I feel stronger and that is not today.

I still don't believe he's gone. I still believe he will walk through that door laden with shopping. I would give absolutely anything to get you back. Anything.

***

I feel a bit better today. The panel for the SI met up yesterday for the hearing, so hopefully this side of the shit fest should be concluded soon.

There was a thunderstorm this evening. Reckon it was Jake throwing shit around.

I don't like thunderstorms without him being here.

✳✳✳

Jake's son messaged me last night... Asking for the password for Sky Sports. Forgot I was still paying for that.

I suppose I should be grateful he at least asked before he tried to use it.

He asks if I'm okay.

'I'm fine,' I say.

✳✳✳

My toothbrush had moved from its usual place this morning. It wasn't me.

The washing up bowl we had in our kitchen sink is massive. As I am mainly eating bread-based goods, I haven't got heaps of washing up so I ordered a new one which should be slightly smaller.

It has turned up today. It is Sylvanian Family sized. Fucking dimensions.

I keep making little changes to the house, trying to make space.

I have become quite resourceful. Jake would be shook.

I don't know why I am trying to make space when there is a giant fucking void in my life already.

Maybe it is the grief equivalent of 'nesting' when you're expecting.

✳✳✳

Went to Polly's today with Mum and Dad as it is Fathers' Day. I hate Sundays now in any event.

It was lovely seeing my niece for the first time since Christmas. She's got so grown up. She was rocking a crop top, mini skirt and fishnets look today. She's fourteen going on twenty-three.

A bird shit on my brother-in-law's shoulder (we blamed Jake) and Mother almost stacked it walking up the drive. Again, we blamed Jake.

I am stoic with my mum and dad. For them. They don't realise how I really feel. I don't share it with them. They're old and I feel I should protect them.

I am raging that Jake hasn't sent me a 'sign'. I keep asking him.

My neighbour is back at home now. I haven't spoken to her as of yet. Her son has told me she doesn't know I am aware she tried to commit suicide.

Mum and Dad are about to 'shield' for a second time due to Covid. I am pleased both of them still work part-time.

I worry about my dad in particular as he suffered a heart attack a few years back and the job he does is quite physical especially when you're in your seventies.

I feel so emotional today. I cannot imagine a life without Jake so I stop imagining it and talk to him incessantly. He's much less opinionated these days.

I wish I could kiss his sweet but weathered face again, squidge his earlobes and ruffle his cress head and bash him on the elbow with the remote control so he could say I was trying to give him elbow cancer.

I have Jake's nieces and a couple of my sisters-in-law over tomorrow for a socially distanced garden party as it's Polly's birthday this week.

✳✳✳

Jesus Christ. Well, that was utter carnage. We got completely sideways.

I did Jake proud though and the food was pretty damn good.

I should've known it'd be a day/night to remember when the girls brought over a bottle of sambuca for Polly!

She passed out on the floor next to an open tub of hummus. I took her into my bedroom to sleep it off and she promptly chucked her guts up. I left her to fester.

Sister-in-law then stacked in down my steps and frozen peas were applied to the area in an attempt to fix her. I called Polly's husband to come pick her up as she was not in a good way and I reckoned she needed her own bed.

The rest of the girls left and I went to bed.

***

Woke up to what looks like an addict's drug hut, but with food and drink instead of heroin. Goals.

It's going to be a long day. It transpires my sister-in-law broke her ankle last night. I also left the freezer door open (fucking peas) and everything has started to defrost. Bollocks.

It gets worse. I started looking at some pictures on my phone of the soiree this weekend and when I zoom in, I can see some images. Looks like angel wings near my bedroom door and some orbs.

It also smells faintly of red wine in the bedroom. Not where Polly vommed as she wasn't drinking red and I've cleaned that up properly.

I sent the pictures to my best mate and she has insisted she calls me as she needs to speak to me urgently.

She has noticed there are a few anomalies on the pictures I've sent her and one of the images is fucking scary. Looks like a demonic face near my front door. It's horrible.

She calls me and makes me do a blessing over the phone with her. I am going round each room with a white candle and a small ramekin of olive oil, drawing crosses on each window and door in the house, saying protection prayers each time I make a cross using the olive oil (expensive too.

Can't use bloody veg oil apparently).

Jake would be absolutely pissing himself.

Once the 'ritual' is over, Charley tells me I am safe but we need to do this just in case. She thinks Jake would have protected me anyway. She bollocks me for doing a ouija board whilst drunk as that can let bad spirits in.

Well, that was June 2020. Off you fuck.

July 2020

I am struggling this week. I have been thinking about my friend losing her husband. She has a little girl and I just know how she must be feeling and it makes me so sad. I suppose at least it keeps my mind off the ongoing investigation at the hospital.

It's a strange old time at the moment. Part of me does feel at least wherever Jake is, on a fluffy cloud or a big beautiful star, that he is safe. Unlike all us fuckers avoiding people literally like we have the plague. Apart from when we're drunk then no fucks are given.

Cora has just let me know her partner Doug has incurable cancer. I've spoken to both of them. To be fair, he sounds not too bad and she's on the vino so is chatting shit.

I ask Jake to look after them and say a little prayer.

Pubs reopen tomorrow. Jake and me would one hundred percent have been heading to the pub! I am avoiding it. Not because I'm scared but because my liver is shot to bits after last weekend.

I am a saint.

I also keep reminding myself that if Jake had survived the operation and would have been on dialysis, we wouldn't have been going out to pubs etc. We'd have been locked up here safe and sound, probably with him wanting to murder me.

I keep seeing a robin in the back garden; he is there all the time. Is it you, Jake? Do you see robins in the summer?

I keep chatting to him anyway and feeding him cheese and bread. Polly is scared I will capture him and try to keep him inside.

***

I had a good cry last night. I felt I needed to hear his voice and played some videos of Jake. It was so lovely to hear his voice but I am so desperate to see him and hold him.

Decided it would help if I ate a giant fish finger baguette.

It did not.

***

I spoke to the coroners today. The deadline for the hospital to have submitted their reports was Monday. Apparently, according to the coroners, the hospital has requested an extension to 14th July. I am also waiting to find out what the reports say in the SI.

It's all coming at once.

Cora's Doug really is not good. I am trying my best to be supportive but I am finding it very hard.

I am still not in the best place and dealing with other's

issues does not come easy at the moment. I ask Jake to make sure Doug doesn't go to Jake's new home yet and to pray for him.

✷✷✷

Chased the trust today and spoke to the lead investigator who has told me the report is now written and approved by the panel and will be presented at corporate governance next week.

Once that happens, the report will go to the commissioners (who are external from the trust). She then told me that once this happens, she will arrange for us to meet up and she will share the report with me plus some 'experts'.

I let the family know. I've said I'd like one of them to come with me but said that this person will need to be reasonable/level-headed/balanced/sensible and not aggy. I've told them I better look outside of the family!

I'm hoping either Bob or Liz will come as they are the most balanced!

I have not stopped today. The Lollipops are coming over tomorrow for our first outing since the pandemic. I am not sure if I am excited or scared!

I cannot stop cleaning or organising shit. It is very different to my usual slovenly self. It must be the grief.

I have treated myself to a manicure this evening. The salon I go to is quite nice and I think they must have struggled through lockdown. I have a nice coral colour for the summer.

The girls come over. We sit in the garden for a wine or two and decide we should wear wigs. We bought them a couple of weeks ago after we did a 'drag night' video call and Lola was wearing an epic pink creation, so ordered me and Trixie the same style (subtle it ain't): one in like a grey/purple (mine) and the other blue. Some rather spectacular pics are taken but to be honest it's fucking thirty degrees and it's not really wig friendly weather.

Wigs discarded, we nip over to the pub for some lunch and more wine. It is boiling. The waiter brings some ice-cold rose for Trixie, a large gin for Lola and a bottle of Malbec for me. It is so hot outside that the wine is lukewarm and I cannot even feel it going down my throat!

I manage though.

We spend a couple of hours in the pub (actually, not in the pub but outside as you are not allowed inside yet, plus it's about ninety degrees) then we go back to mine. I get out the dips and crisps. Fortunately, they are aware I'm not a cook so they do not expect a Jake special.

I don't go too nuts today as Polly and me are going to see Jake's family tomorrow for more drinks, and I feel I haven't seen them for way too long.

Jake's brother picks us up the following day. I've given him a few of Jake's shirts and tops as they're roughly the same size. I have stipulated though if he doesn't want them that he needs to give them back to me and not give them away or bin them. I haven't got rid of any of his clothes other than his newish puffer jacket that I gave to his son and told him the same thing.

We all pile in to Bob's for drinks in the garden. It is lovely to see them all. One of my sisters-in-law is already utterly clattered and very emotional and the other one did a pole dance round the garden umbrella.

Standard behaviour.

Bob's playing some decent tunes. When mine and Jake's wedding song comes on, I must have zoned out but my sister-in-law's cousin's husband (brother's, dog's, and budgie) is calling my name and just asks me if I am okay. I do not really know him well, but his concern touches me.

'I'm fine,' I say.

✳✳✳

After such a busy few days, I have decided to try to get my head into order. I need to start telling people I am not okay.

I was looking at some pictures on my phone of Jake and my sister. They were taken the week before the operation. They're silly Snapchat ones. It broke my heart looking at them with the knowledge that just a few days later, I lost him.

I wish that this knot in my chest would dissipate, but it doesn't. Ever.

I think I've got one sided Covid. One side of my face aches, my ears and throat hurt.

Told you I was dramatic.

The following day, my Covid seems to have gone away.

This weekend, I am going to the garden centre with Polly and Dave. Need to sort my back garden out as it looks like shit. Spend £230 on plants and pots. I'm trying to create a little sanctuary for me and Jake when the weather is nice.

Have another video call with Trixie this evening and we have a couple of drinks, but once it's over, I feel so sad. It's not been a good day. I end the day crying myself into a fitful sleep.

I wake up in the middle of the night, look through some more pictures of Jake, enlarge them on my phone and kiss each one of them. It makes me feel better; tomorrow I want to wake up not wanting to die.

August 2020

I have to give a statement to the coroners today, talking about his life, any illnesses and the impact of his death. That was nice.

I wasn't prepared for this. I didn't have a clue I would need to do this.

It's like they just want me to keep bringing everything up again and again. It's torture.

They don't make it easy for people.

How do they think it has affected me and the family?

Good grief. Finally get the date through for my meeting with the trust and the SI on 20th August. I am gripped by anticipation and fear at the same time. I have been waiting for this for a ridiculous amount of time. I didn't think it would happen.

If I'm being truthful, all the time I didn't know how Jake died, I could pretend he wasn't actually really properly dead. It's a bit like the build up to the funeral. You put it off so you don't have to deal with any realities.

∗∗∗

The day of the meeting arrives. I've booked a taxi to the hospital. Mainly because I'm a lazy bitch but also because

I really can't trust myself to make it there without turning around and coming back home.

The taxi journey will take approximately thirty minutes. This will be the first time I have had to go back to the hospital since Jake died.

The taxi driver is really sweet. He tells me that he hopes my appointment is nothing serious and I end up explaining a little of why I am going to the hospital. Weirdly enough, sometimes it is easier telling a stranger than going over it again with people I am close to. The taxi driver tells me how he split from his wife a few years back but it was all very friendly and they've remained close. He tells me she was the love of his life.

Liz is going to meet me at the hospital. I sit on a wall outside of the hospital, have a cigarette and call my sister. I am about forty-five minutes too early. Story of my life.

I am absolutely bricking it.

I spot Liz and we walk in, greeted by our rep. She is very friendly and we begin the long walk to the other side of the hospital making small talk along the way.

Finally, we arrive at the room where the meeting will be held. There's a man and another two women already in there.

They introduce themselves. We have a vascular surgeon, the head of nursing and another nurse, plus Carole who has been dealing with Jake's case.

It seems formal. Carole is chairing the meeting. The

surgeon begins by explaining the rationale behind electing for the original operation. He goes on to explain the complexities the team had to try to handle during the operation. He says that the whereabouts of the aneurysm plus very high BP resulted in a huge amount of complications that nobody could have foreseen nor prevented. Each time a problem occurred, another issue arose.

Although the coroners refer to heart disease in their preliminary investigations, the surgeon has explained that it refers to the aneurysm as this is basically heart disease. It's just unfortunate wording.

I feel reassured that absolutely everything that could have been done was done but ultimately his heart couldn't take anymore strain.

In the meeting, Liz told the team she didn't think he would survive the operation.

This is news to me. This devastates me. More than what the professionals are telling me. She was his sister. How could you let somebody go through this if you thought they wouldn't come out the other end? I am dumbstruck. But do you know what I do? I hold her hand whilst she sobs.

I am fine.

The head of nursing takes her turn to speak; she covers the care of Jake once he came into ICU.

One of the items she talks about is the resuscitation. She explains that whilst it is protocol to ask the next of kin if they wish to attend, the nursing staff should set the scene and explain what you will likely witness so you are prepared.

I was not. I was just asked if I wanted to attend the resuscitation and see him and obviously I did.

I was fragile. Nothing could have prepared me for the scene. It was horrendous.

I ask her why you are given an option to attend a resuscitation. She explains that some relatives want to see that everything is being done and that it may help in the long term.

In my opinion, this is madness but perhaps it is just me.

She tells me she is so sorry. She says that when she read what I went through, she cried as she could understand the pain and realised it was not handled in the best way.

She says, because of this, they are firming up on their training with their nursing staff to make sure lessons are learnt and others don't have the same experience.

There are a few things they are implementing after some of the questions I raised but this is mainly to do with family aftercare so if I can help others at least something more positive could come out of it.

Now we just have the coroners' inquest to deal with then the formalities are over.

Liz and I walk towards the town. We decide we should eat something and add a bottle of Malbec to the order of chips.

She goes home by bus and I wait for the train. I feel relieved, sad and bewildered all at the same time.

It's so hot today and there's no shade at the station. I sit and roast and nurse an impending headache.

Later that day, whilst thinking about Jake, I remember the tarot reading I had. I remember she said, 'He wants you to let go of something that is imprisoning you.' I think he was referring to the inquests and investigations and he wants me to let go.

So, I'm letting go. I feel a rendition of *Frozen* coming up.

∗∗∗

Meet Trixie for a boozy lunch today. We trot off to the Italian and line our stomachs with something with pasta and salmon for me and something with sausage and pasta for Trixie, plus rose, of course. Oh, and garlic bread.

The boozy lunch turns into a boozy pub crawl and ends up with us both in my garden with many twinkly lights and more wine and crisps for sustenance.

I have a habit of taking random videos of any event and watching them the following day to see how much of a prick I have been or whether or not I have grown up. Evidently, I have not.

I love my girlfriends.

September 2020

Greg and Natalie are coming over today to sort out my front garden which is completely knackered.

I have tried to get into gardening but I don't like insects and unless it's watering or pruning, I cannot be bothered. Greg has got hold of some sleepers at trade price and is going to put those in and re-gravel it etc.

Me and Natalie will supervise whilst drinking rose, I suspect.

They turn up about 11 a.m., get right on to the garden and Greg has brought a case of Stella. Thirsty work this gardening shiz.

I am clearly not doing anything but make endless trips to the fridge and back handing out 'refreshments'. Natalie and me end up sitting in my back garden drinking wine whilst Greg does his stuff out the front.

After about four or five hours, it's sorted. It looks really good so I take them over to the pub for a late lunch. We have a nice platter (of course) and plenty of wine.

We go back to mine, sit in the garden and, to be honest, apart from flashing my boobs at Greg, I don't remember much. They crashed at mine.

***

This morning, we are looking through the pics of last night and they're not horrendous but Greg reminds me he promised he would turn my life around. He then proceeds to swap round the fridge door which has always opened the wrong way.

This is life changing (according to Greg). It will now take me about seven years to get used to it opening the right way. He also uses a hammer at 8 a.m. I'm sure my neighbours are thrilled.

✳✳✳

Cora calls me to tell me her Doug has died.

At the moment, she sounds okay. I think she knew he was going. I am so sad for her. We arrange to speak later on.

✳✳✳

A Sunday lunchtime session with Trixie and Lola today. We're off to Turtle Bay for lunch and cocktails

It escalated from lunchtime to a full day and night's worth of drinking.

Luckily, I am off tomorrow.

✳✳✳

The final inquest is today. All online due to Covid.

I am due to dial in soon and I'm dreading it.

God, it was so formal. I wasn't prepared for that. They

obviously spoke in tremendous detail about the whole event, the operation, the death, the post-mortem and finally the verdict.

It's now over. No more formalities, thank God, but raking over the incident is so painful and because these were coroners, they left no stone unturned.

I need a drink.

October 2020

Polly and I have arranged to go out for dinner with Sienna and Ashleen for what would have been my twelfth wedding anniversary to Jake.

We get pictures sent to our WhatsApp group of the girls drinking wine in the car on the way here. Going to be one of those nights.

They come round to mine about 6 o'clock. We get the wine out, and the table at a nice Italian place is booked for 7:30 p.m.

The girls tell me we won't be walking as they're wearing heels so they call an Uber. I quickly change from boots to high shoes now I know we're not walking. The Uber comes and then says the four of us can't travel due to Covid. The max is three. We book a local taxi which turns up just in time and we pile in. No Covid rules there. Weird.

The evening starts with Sienna taking a pic of me and it is a side on picture as she wanted to highlight the fact my mask is wrapped around my ear showing it off and making it look absolutely massive.

We sit at the table and a young waiter turns up to ask if we'd like to order drinks. Poor fucker, he looks terrified as Sienna is winding him right up. I see that once he takes our drink order, he is pulled aside by who I would assume would be the manager of the place. Our waiter is replaced by what I can only call a complete snack, all big glistening teeth, a Mediterranean god with a big flirty personality. I can see what they did there!

Sienna asks him if he'd peel her prawn.

He asks what the occasion is and I clam up. Sienna says, 'Just loving life,' and cheers everyone.

Two more bottles of wine between us and only Ashleen eats her food.

Back to mine.

Out pops the coke!

Fuck's sake. Why do I keep doing this?

We all rap to Eminem. Why?

***

I've arranged to meet up with my old boss. We worked together for years. He's a little older than me, married with an adolescent son.

We arrange to meet in The Stoke so only stone's throw for me, which is good as it is pissing down.

Now this is weird. I've known Jason for years. We have always had a flirty banter type relationship. It's kind of just how I am. I am standing looking at myself and immediately need to reassess the outfit. I'm currently wearing a loose silk tunic top, pretty triple strand pendant and black not so skinnies and heels. I feel I am too dressed up and will give him the wrong idea.

Tuck tunic in, add massive chunky belt and change into my patent DMs (impulse buy, felt hard). I feel I need a protective barrier around me so the DMs are good. I take off the necklace and rub off my lippy.

For fuck's sake.

Right, I'm ready now. I cross over the road and walk into the pub. It's fairly busy.

We are currently in the 'rule of six' debacle so there are a few groups of six or less people dotted about and it is table service at the pub. I am a fan of this.

I order a small glass of rose and plonk myself on a table with high stools. I hate being here first and I hate walking into a pub on my tod. I hate having to be a grown-up.

Jason turns up five minutes later. I ask him if he wants to 'embrace'. Em fucking brace… what? Cunt. I hate myself already. He says we better not due to Covid shit. He orders a coke as he's driving and he asks me how I am.

Obviously, I say I am fine. Then he asks a few questions about what happened and I find myself elaborating, but rather than feeling teary and emotional, I am being very straightforward and forceful. I know what I am doing. I don't want to feel vulnerable so I seem to have created this hard woman persona. It's not me at all. I am as soft as shit.

He listens and I carry on for ages and he doesn't interrupt or ask any questions, just sits there and listens to me banging on.

Eventually, the pub gets too busy so we pop over the road. This is the pub where we had Jake's after party. It's the first time I have been in there. We sit outside in a covered area. The heaters are on and, to be honest, it isn't cold.

We chat for a little bit and he buys me another wine and some nibbles. I tell him my bum's gone numb and get up to go to the loo. He tells me it's because my bum's disappeared.

People keep telling me I have lost weight but I don't see it. Anyway, that makes me feel better.

He keeps eluding to the fact he isn't happy with his wife. So, I make sure I keep talking about Jake. I am constantly looking around making sure no one is looking at us as a couple. How would they know? How would I fucking know that they thought that?

This is completely exhausting.

We stay for another hour and say goodbye without any embracing!

I literally run home. I found that a bit of a chore. It wasn't Jason. It was me trying to be someone I am most certainly not.

It's Halloween and I'm meeting Patricia, Liz and Rachel at Wetherspoons for a spot of lunch and some drinks.

I rock up to Spoons in town and the ladies are already sat at a table.

There's a bit of a weird atmosphere to begin with. Not sure why. Both Patricia and Liz tell me I have lost too much weight and that I am looking scrawny. Impossible.

We have a nice lunch. All picky bits full of calories and carbs. It seems I have drunk the bar dry of red wine as they try to offload some wine *on tap*! Oh, fuck off, there aren't any bottles left! Ridiculous.

Patricia is on form as ever. She has fashioned a napkin as a headpiece and also puts our other sister (Jo: the alcoholic) on loud speaker in an attempt to bring her into the mix, but we're drunk and she ends up cutting her off.

Also, Liz farts and it is absolutely disgusting.

I'm home before 6 p.m. and switch on YouTube and listen to George Michael before falling asleep on the sofa.

This was a fairly tame meet up. I can't help feeling a bit disappointed.

Lockdown for us all again from today.

November 2020

Me and Polly are having a little soiree this evening.

We keep dressing up and doing our hair and make up despite the fact that we can't go 'out out'.

We just listen to shit eighties music and dance away. Polly tries to add a bit of Eminem or Amy Whitehouse but I usually win the battle of the music.

✳✳✳

This morning, we use the Just Eat app to order a massive McDonalds for us both plus Dave.

They accept the order and we get confirmation about forty-five minutes later that the delivery is on its way.

There is a tracking page which shows a little man on a bike currently sat at the traffic lights after about five minutes.

The excitement is real. Haven't had a McDonalds for a very long time.

After about twenty minutes of constantly refreshing the tracking page, the little man appears to have fucked off with our lunch. All of a sudden, it tells us that they were unable to deliver to us.

We contact the 'help' page which is absolutely laughable and explain the situation and they say the driver attempted to deliver the food but couldn't. We advised the operator that we have not only been in all this morning, we have pretty much had our noses stuck to the fucking window waiting for this melt to turn up with our quarter pounders. Pricks.

We ask if they can reorder and redeliver and they say they can't and I need to raise a complaint to get the money back.

Motherfuckers.

We're all sad and dejected, so once Polly and Dave leave, I console myself by making a toasted cheese sandwich with an accompaniment of Wotsits followed by some porridge with a couple of Lindors chucked in it to make it all chocolatey.

Get my refund from Just Eat. Smart.

I have a video call scheduled this evening with Lola and Trixie. The theme is film.

I decide to be an Oompa Loompa. I have a green wig and yellow face paint plus I have a wicked jumpsuit in bright yellow animal print, so that'll do.

***

The following morning, I am tidying up and I have two small but very heavy silver pineapples that I love. Jake hated them. They are knocked over onto a mirrored tray. If I did it, I would have a hundred percent heard the thud. Is this a sign?

When I wrote in my journal last night before I went to bed, I asked Jake to give me a sign.

Maybe this was a sign?

✳✳✳

Lola and Trixie are again breaking lockdown rules and coming over today to help me decorate my Christmas tree. I decide this year I should do something to mark Christmas.

I really don't want to but Jake made Christmas so brilliant for me that it seems the right thing to do.

We have blown up airbeds ready as previous efforts have failed as we are usually way too drunk.

We have a lovely time and the girls do most of the work while I do what I do best which is manage the refreshments.

We order a massive Domino's: one doner kebab pizza (don't knock it till you try it) and a pepperoni, plus garlic bread and dips.

Bloody great night plus Trixie has brought over some puddings!

December 2020

How the actual fuck is it December? Lockdown has ended and been replaced with a tier system.

It's so bloody confusing. We're in tier 2 at the moment. This means we can go out in a group of no more than six people and it's all table service. No issues with that. So, I've organised 'Jake Day' for 12th December to mark the day I lost him.

***

Charley has booked me in to see a medium: a well-known psychic in North Cheam. I was shocked this wasn't cancelled but I called him and he explained there is a Perspex screen between us (obviously the virus can't go up and over the screen) plus the room we'll be in is well ventilated and roomy.

This morning, three lightbulbs blew. Surely this is a sign.

I am so nervous. Not nervous at seeing the medium, just terrified Jake won't come through and talk to me.

Charley manages to find a place to park pretty much right outside the house and we sit and chain smoke for about thirty minutes as we're early.

Time to go in now. I knock and he answers. He reminds me of Gary Glitter the Thailand years. All white hair and pointy goatee.

Obviously, we don't shake hands and there's no elbow bump and anyway I immediately apologise as I desperately need to have a wee. That's the bloody coffee and fags.

He directs me upstairs and once I have been for a wee and washed my hands, I make my way down.

He doesn't ask me anything other than whether or not 'I believe'. To which I immediately start to waffle on about my obsession with all things paranormal to which he actually tells me to be quiet as he has someone who wants to talk to me.

Jake comes through and was obnoxious and rude and just how I love him. The medium laughs throughout as Jake keeps dropping the c bomb (don't know why I have written that as this book has a liberal sprinkling of cunt throughout).

He is frighteningly accurate, referring to me giving Jake's watch to his son recently, about red wine and music and he is talking to me like Jake would talk to me.

The medium also says Jake is a cocky fucker. This makes me laugh out loud as he couldn't be more right.

I have recorded the session. I am absolutely blown away.

Me and Charley listen to the recording in the car on

the way home. She is flabbergasted too.

The medium told me there are never any guarantees loved ones will come through but as he was saying that, he started smiling and said, 'But I don't think we'll have that problem today.' He told me there was man with us and he was picking up that he passed quite quickly. He said he was a bit of a joker and a piss- taking bastard.

He asked if Jake's lifestyle choices may have contributed to his passing and frankly that is pretty accurate. He said Jake is laughing at what we're doing as it's all a load of bollocks! That's exactly what he'd have said. A hundred percent.

He said the virus would not have kept him in and that he's a right little fucker. He said Jake would not have played ball.

The medium asked me if his body just shut down. Yes. Did he drink a bit? Yes. Did his dad have a lung condition? Yes, he had asbestosis which attributed to his death.

He mentioned various names I don't recognise. He asks about a Marta: that's my mum's name or Jake's ex-wife. Awkward.

He kept laughing saying Jake is laughing. He told me Jake's dad likes me too and that the pair of them aren't 'old' people. That's true. Both were no age when they passed.

He then referred to Jake's nickname. I can't tell you this as it is too personal but it is so obscure I know now one hundred percent that he was there. He was trying to get

Jake's name and goes through John and a James before he said, 'He's telling me, "Tell her, it's fucking Jake"!'

He mentioned a lost wedding ring. I can't find Jake's wedding ring.

He also said Jake was saying he knew I was with him when he was in hospital and that I was making a fuss as usual and kept covering up his legs and feet (which I did). Jake told the medium to tell me that he was all right and he knows I kissed him on his head.

He asked if Jake's body shut down with his kidneys failing. Then asked who Bob is; he was saying hello to Bob. That's his brother.

He then asked me if I was wearing his clothes. Ummm yes. Have I given his watch to his son? Yes.

The medium asked me if I have Jake's ashes at home. Yes.

To be honest, there was a shit load more that he said but I can't really elaborate as it's so specific and I can't give the real names etc. away. But if you get the chance and you believe, please consider seeing him. He is simply amazing.

It lifts my spirits no end and I feel like I have spent time with him and that makes me so happy.

✳✳✳

I have got an evening round Cora's organised this evening. I really can't be arsed as she does my head in but she's going through a lot. I think she likes to talk to me as I know what she is going through, but it's different. All grief is different. All grief is painful but she knew Doug was dying. She knew for a long time he was going to die. Does that make it easier? No, but the shock is taken away and that was a big thing for me.

She insists I try a Rioja that she has in her wine rack. It's the only red wine I am not keen on but clearly, I'll try it… to appease her obviously.

I'm only there for three hours but we manage to demolish three bottles of wine between us so I get a cab home.

I fall asleep on the sofa and wake up at 1:30 a.m.

✳✳✳

Me and Polly have got tattoos booked on 'Jake Day'. I'm clearly still embracing my mid-life crisis.

Polly has a lovely tattoo behind her ear and I have something in memory of my man, obvs.

We then meet up with Greg and Natalie at Turtle Bay. We booked for 2 p.m. for a bottomless brunch.

I am paranoid the staff will ask if we all live in one home as the lockdown rules are changing daily and you're not supposed to socialise outside of 'your bubble'.

They don't ask a thing and we have a blast. There's so many raised glasses to Jake and I love it.

The bill is paid by Greg and we did the bottomless brunch a service!

We walk back to mine stopping on the way into the little shop down the road. Greg picks up some cigs (as he has been smoking mine), a couple of bottles of wine and some snacks.

We go back to mine and basically sing and dance as is standard. I think Greg and Natalie leave about 2 a.m.

Good grief.

∗∗∗

I look through my phone and there are a few pretty excellent videos of us all almost stacking it as we're dancing around. My favourite one though is a picture of Natalie who has pulled her knickers down and mooned and you can pretty much see her fanny.

This is why we are friends.

∗∗∗

I meet Lola for a boozy lunch. Do I actually do anything else? This book started off being a self-help book for others who are dealing with grief, but it's turned into a journal of my alcoholic tendencies. Fuck's sake.

Anyway, we do go out and we go to The Cosy Club. I wasn't sure how I'd feel about going there as it was a place that me and Jake frequented.

Me and Lola pose as sisters, obviously due to Covid rules. We're seated and we're sitting down and as we're chatting, the light above us starts to flicker. We were talking about Jake. Clearly another sign.

Drunkenness ensues.

Me and Lola go to bed at 3:30 a.m. after re-enacting the Madonna 'Like a Prayer' video.

She is Jesus and I am Madonna. Widow trumps all.

Two days later, Boris puts us into Tier 4 and cancels Christmas.

Luckily for me, as I'm in a bubble with Polly, I am okay but we can't risk seeing Mum and Dad which is very sad.

We hatch a plan that Mum and Dad will pick me up Christmas morning and take me to Polly's. They'll stay in the car and see Polly plus Dave and Nicole through the window and deliver and receive presents.

Well, this is all bollocks, isn't it? Polly calls me and says Dave is feeling a bit ropey.

This is the day before Christmas Eve. She says he's waiting to get a test tomorrow but won't get the results until after Christmas.

In the words of The Clash: should I stay or should I go?

Clearly, I'm going. What else can I do? I'm not staying on my own on Christmas Day. Fuck that.

***

So, Christmas Day comes. Dave does get his results back but they are inconclusive so he needs to be tested again!

I get picked up by the olds and they do as we asked and stay in the car. I grab their presents and take them to their car and they give me Nicole's presents and there's just lots of frantic hand waving before they leave and head home.

Time to start Christmas then.

Obviously, sherry is the first port of call. Nicole has a glass as well. Dave seems fine. If he has Covid, he's hiding it well.

We make sure we eat dinner for a change which was gorgeous but we're hammered and it goes from bad to worse.

Dave starts making cocktails for the girls. Now, bear in mind, we've already polished off two bottles of sherry between me and Polly (giving Nicole the occasional glass). We start with a nice one. Can't remember what the hell it was but it tasted nice. The one that threw us off kilter was a Manhattan. It was vile. Polly and Nicole only had a sip but I hate waste so I drank theirs too.

I tell Dave to not put alcohol in Nicole's but I think he's pissed as well so he's knocking them out.

It ends up with Nicole lying on the sofa pretty much comatose vomiting into a bowl. See the similarity of last Christmas? There is a theme.

I can't watch this so I go into the kitchen and watch Dave prepare more cocktails for me and Polly.

Once Nicole cannot be any more sick, he carries her up to bed.

We then stop drinking cocktails. Polly stops drinking entirely as she is concerned about Nicole and Dave switches to brandy and I hit the wine.

We decide to watch a Christmassy type film: *The Exorcist.*

Happy Christmas all.

***

I'm working between Christmas and New Year (27th to 31st December) and Polly calls me on 27th to let me know she is doing a test as Dave's test result has come back positive so I need to take a test.

I order a test online and it comes via Amazon later that day. Pretty impressive.

***

I do the test and send it off for the results on 28th Dec. Polly's results come back positive.

I feel fine.

***

It's 30th December and I wake up feeling delirious, freezing cold, boiling hot, shivering, sweating. The whole kit and caboodle. Luckily, work isn't busy but as I'm the only one in over Christmas, I soldier on.

Polly and me cancel our plans for NYE as we both feel under the weather.

January 2021

Test results came back today: positive. Happy New Year. Fuck off.

On the bright side, I see in the New Year without a hangover. This is big news.

I've bought loads of goodies for New Year and I'm devastated as my baked camembert and all the trimmings taste of fuck all. I cannot taste a thing.

I ate a Whispa too. It tasted of velvet air. Gutted.

Hateful Covid.

I do not mind feeling fluey but I draw the line at not being able to taste anything.

It has taken about ten days before I can actually smell my shampoo, so I think my senses might me coming back (not as in common sense, obviously).

I have a video call planned with the girls this weekend and drink my first drink since Christmas Day (goals).

I consume a bottle of wine, chat shit with the girls, then Greg calls so I open the Baileys and have a glass or three of that.

I wake up at 3 a.m., fire still blazing, surrounded by cheesy Nik Naks that I was obviously trying to eat at one stage. The sleeves of my roll neck top are round by my neck. Think I must've got hot and tried to take my top off.

Back to my best. Normal business has been resumed.

✱✱✱

I walked into the kitchen this morning. It was dark as it was early and I turned the spotlights on under the kitchen cupboards and none of them worked. There was an odd vibration coming from a knife holder on the opposite side of the kitchen. No idea what it was but clearly it was a sign from Jake. I wish he'd just come to bed but guess it makes sense he's hanging around in the kitchen as that was the place he most frequented!

I feel I'm due a good old cry soon. Kind of feel a bit suppressed and my chest aches. Probably a combination of 'rona, cigs and grief.

✱✱✱

I got woken up really early today. Not sure why but then I went into the kitchen and looked out the window and what do you know… it was snowing. It was a thing we had together that he would always wake me up if it was snowing or somebody famous had died. Guessing no one famous has popped their clogs.

Another video call sesh this evening with the Lollipops. We're dressing up as 'women who inspire us'. I'm going as Trixie as she is an inspiration, plus she has big hair and wears animal print.

Hair is currently in rollers and I'm looking at my eye pencils seeing which one's best to draw on some freckles!

This is what lockdown has done to us all!

I wake up this morning and I have a scratch down my forehead. WTF. Demon?

Jake wouldn't hurt me.

I've invited Mum and Dad over tomorrow as, although we shouldn't be seeing each other, I think they're desperate. They've been locked up for weeks.

I am making them nachos.

I still keep thinking how the hell I'd have kept Jake in during lockdown. It would have been so hard. He'd have murdered, for sure. So, to make up for that, I keep chatting to him asking if he can eat and drink anything he fancies up there, tell him that's pretty smart if that's fact as I am still trying to battle off the Christmas fatness.

I pretty much disinfect the entire house in preparation of the olds' visit tomorrow, getting rid of any germs. That makes it sound like I'm a slovenly bitch. I'm not. I've cleaned incessantly since Jake went. It keeps me occupied.

***

Cora keeps calling me wanting to talk. I realise in her eyes it makes sense that she calls on me as I have been through the same scenario. But sometimes I don't want to hear her pain. I haven't addressed mine yet and I don't feel equipped being her grief counsellor until I am in a better place. I try to speak to her when I can but she's so angry at Doug and I'm not angry with Jake. I'm just really sad.

She also has a habit of bringing up Jake and her, even though they were literally just fuck buddies for a few months decades ago. I quite literally want to throat punch her sometimes.

Another video sesh tomorrow with the girls. Obvs a theme: animals. Think we're running out of ideas!

I decide today I am going to write a book about Jake and everything that has happened since.

✳✳✳

I had the weirdest dream last night. I dreamt Jake was around and we were discussing how now was the right time to start telling people he was actually alive and how we were going to handle the fallout.

It was almost unbearable when I woke up and realised he wasn't here and it was all a dream.

Polly's coming over tomorrow evening to celebrate New Year (as we couldn't on NYE as she had Covid) and I can't wait to see her. I spoke to Cora this evening and she asked what I'm doing tomorrow so I told her Polly's coming over.

She asked me if I had any booze in. I replied, 'Of course I have. I'm Jake's wife,' and laughed. She responded with a giggle and said, 'Yes and I was his girlfriend.'

I just went silent. I'm only not biting because she's hurting and hurt people hurt people.

I message her in the week to tell her we can't talk every Friday as it's too draining. Well, actually, if I'm honest, I don't tell her that exactly. I've said I just want to keep weekends free and not commit to every Friday. She seems to have taken it okay. I can't keep putting myself through all the emotional turmoil. Sometimes you've got to be a bit selfish and put your own needs before others.

Work has gone crazy. It's so busy but that's good as it's keeping me focused.

Oh, for the love of God. Polly and I have our little fake NYE party. We so want to be edgy and cool but we end up singing to The Carpenters' 'Calling Occupants' and Patti Labelle and Michael McDonald's 'On My Own'. We also tried to practise slut drops and various other dance moves.

February 2021

I'm fucking miserable today and my dinner is crap. Hangry.

***

Call with the Lollipops this evening. We're going as Boy George. I'm currently plaiting tiny strands of multi-coloured hair extensions and have bought myself a grey fedora.

I've also eaten porridge with a mini Snickers bar in it and for lunch, homemade chicken nugs and chips. It is fat Saturday after all.

Had a cracking call with the Pops and Cora tried to call me while I was on the phone to them.

I called her back. She was clearly drunk and I was definitely on my way. She was banging on about how angry she was at Doug and his dying. She kept asking me why I wasn't angry at Jake and I said I couldn't be angry with him as I know he didn't want to leave me. She was being so negative that, in the end, I said I couldn't relate to how she was feeling and she said maybe tonight wasn't the right time to talk and kind of hung up on me. Bummer.

Seems crazy to think that Jake's funeral was a year ago. It seems like forever ago but like yesterday all at the same time. I can't explain it.

I can't seem to get him out of my head. I look around my front room and there are pictures everywhere of Jake. I've got the two cushions of his beautiful face and I've got his ashes in a box displayed on the centre of our sideboard.

Then you walk into the hallway and there is a collage of his pictures hanging up, then off to the bathroom where his toothbrush still stands alongside mine. The majority of his toiletries are packed under the sink but I still have his aftershave — Issey Miyaki — and a couple of odds and sods.

In the kitchen, I have a chopping board saying 'Jake's Kitchen' and a mug with his face on it.

In the bedroom, I have a certificate with a star named after him, our wedding photo and two displays of all his pics.

I also keep his dressing gown hanging up on the back of the door.

Is it any wonder I see him and feel him everywhere?

✳✳✳

It's been a tough month this month. Fuck Valentine's Day and all that bollocks.

You can buy cards to send to loved ones in heaven. There is a market for everything.

Bought some MI5 plants for outside the front door today (obvs Ramzon). MI5 equals basically topiary plants. We watched a lot of *Spooks* and we named them MI5 plants.

It's Valentine's Day today… another one.

Heard Jacket Jackson's 'Together Again' on the radio this morning. I've never really listened to the words although I've sung along to this song a thousand times. It's my song to you, Jake.

When you lose someone you love and who had such an impact on your life, it's so hard and you miss them so much. But, as it goes on, what you also miss is the things that you are now doing that you can't do together.

***

Pancake day today. I made proper pancakes… had to ask Polly for the recipe!

Made them with 'pasta' flour. Who knew.

***

Had a video call with sisters-in-law today. Patricia clocked Jake's cushion behind me and freaked out. She thought it was actually him.

***

My cleaning habit is getting out of hand. I have discovered I can remove the glass from my fake fire. It was very satisfying cleaning the inside of the glass and found a big old cobweb.

It probably won't work when I switch it on again now.

Got Charley and Louise over tomorrow. Probably more paranormal stuff will occur.

Charley's not coming over as she's not feeling too clever after her Covid jab. I still took this afternoon off and sneaked in a little nana nap.

We're slowly coming out of lockdown apparently. I keep reporting the latest to Jake. He must be bored shitless.

I had a long convo with Cora last night and she told me Doug was gambling approximately £600 to £800 per month. She then said that 'our' partners were both gamblers. I let her know Jake only gambled on the big days like Gold Cup day or Grand National and for pennies not hundreds of bloody pounds. She said that he did whilst she was with him. This was almost thirty years ago FFS. She needs to let go.

I have a tin of chickpeas leftover from the panic buying when we first went into lockdown so decide to make some homemade hummus.

I got a recipe and used a little mini blender stick that I didn't know I had. I was scooping out the remnants from inside where the blades are and for some unknown fucking reason, I hit the on button. I felt it hit my finger and immediately thought I'd sliced it off. There was blood and chickpeas all over the kitchen. I immediately felt queasy and grabbed some kitchen roll, wrapped it round my finger and called Polly as I was panicking.

It's okay. I've got a lovely wedge of flesh out of my index finger.

***

My finger is murder.

I am almost in the ten stone bracket. I'm not sure how this has happened. My size 14 clothes are too big.

Polly and I are having a sherry and pizza night tomorrow. Aren't we edgy? Therefore, I will be a fat bastard for the weekend and will likely be filling the size 14 clothes by Monday.

My beautiful Trixie sent me a Ramazon voucher to go towards an outdoor heater.

March 2021

I have a reading with a lady called Michelle today. It's quite similar to my reading with the medium but not quite as specific. Still good though. The main thing is, with both the readings, Jake's character really comes through: domineering and a bit arrogant. Just the way I love him.

✳✳✳

Trixie and Lola were over last night for a sleepover. It was hilarious.

Much wine was consumed. I purchased 'clean wine', or something like that, to add to a bottle of wine that allegedly cancels out the hangover the following day. All bollocks.

I look though our videos and pictures. I was wearing a brunette wig but it is clear from the photos I pulled it off and scraped my hair back. I look deranged and my forehead is absolutely enormous in the manner of Pennywise the clown.

I've looked through YouTube and can see that our playlist consisted of: *The Greatest Showman*, Abba, Ace of Base, Matt Mitchell, The Stereophonics and Gary fucking Glitter. Jesus

April 2021

Polly and I have resorted to wigs and false lashes whenever we go out. It's like we're incognito. This may be a good thing bearing in mind how ridiculous we are.

I've made a rather delicious chilli as Lola and Trixie are over this weekend.

We have the best time. These girls are life. There is much dancing, singing, drinking and smoking.

They both leave earlyish the next morning once I've plied them with coffee and croissants.

For lunch, I have cold leftover chilli (as obviously heating it up in the microwave for two minutes fell out of my capabilities today) with a side of leftover garlic ciabatta and a packet of Frazzles for an additional flavour sensation.

I spend the afternoon feeling like a fat bastard and sleeping off my hangover.

I'm getting paranoid that I am having a 'good life' without Jake.

This is definitely a pattern. Have fun, get drunk, always with company, but once the party is over, I start over-analysing how I feel. Which, to be honest, is usually just drunk.

Lola messaged me once she got home to say she's necked a Berocca to counteract the effects of the alcohol.

I have just found a bar of Terry's chocolate orange which has biscuit pieces in it that Trixie left for me, adding to an already insanely health conscious day.

Trixie's husband has asked her to fuck off back to mine as, so far, she's blown the fuses on her kettle, toaster and washing machine!

Clearly Lola and I feel this must be a sign and therefore paranormal.

I take the empties out the following morning: six bottles of Prosecco, a bottle of vodka (I hope to Christ that wasn't full to begin with) and a bottle of rose. Not too bad as it was pretty much an all-day session.

I've also just looked at my Alexa voice commands. We have as follows:

Alexa, turn it up, you bitch
Alexa, play Whitney throw down
Alexa, play some shed (what?)
Alexa, fuck off

And it also keeps saying, 'audio cannot be recognised'. Maybe slurring?

I decide to change my autumn/winter wardrobe to spring/summer and get the cases down from the top of the wardrobe. Almost break my neck in the process.

Out from the top of the wardrobe falls my vibrator. Hmmmm, another sign.

I also find Jake's old watch with a broken strap.

Then I am looking in my smaller wardrobe and find a travel sized bottle of Durex lube. It is not mine. Me and Jake didn't use lube.

All these signs.

Oh God, it could be my landlord's. A little bit of sick has just come up.

I've been asked to go into the office to do some induction training with a couple of new starters next week. First time in the office for months. I am bricking it but maybe it will be good to push myself out of my comfort zone.

May 2021

Now I only have summer clothes out, it has decided to turn unseasonably cold for May. I've also fucked my neck up, probably from changing said wardrobe over.

I have also just discovered that my toaster has a crumb tray. I have emptied it. The wonders of TikTok.

I'm meeting up with a girl I used to work with in Turtle Bay for a bottomless brunch. She's hardcore and ten years younger than me.

We consume many, many cocktails. My fave is the expresso martini and also a UB40 (because it has red wine in it). We get proper drunk and then go back to mine where I smoke a shed load and then… then we have the audacity to have dinner plus drinks at 9 fucking 30 p.m. in The Cosy Club. Somehow, I make it. Jen was sick on the way home.

Go me!

It's got hot again. So, what best to do on a bank holiday weekend? Paint your bedroom including the wardrobe. Pale grey walls, off-white shabby chic wardrobe and the piece de la resistance pink flamingo stencils.

June 2021

I hate June. Birthday month. I have decided on a quiet affair with the sister.

I am fashioning a maxi dress combi with DMs and a platinum blonde bobbed wig. Polly turns up looking all serene and perfect a la Audrey Hepburn in pale wide leg trousers teamed with a silky wrap top. She looks beautiful. I look like a white Floella Benjamin.

We go to The Cosy Club for snacks and drinks.

We order a jug of sangria and ask that there is no ice added. This is because:

- Sensitive teeth
- More alcohol

It backfires as they arrive with our jug of sangria which is fucking tiny as it isn't bulked up with ice. Our plan is a fail. Pricks. It's my birthday.

We have a lovely night and end up, as we usually do, dancing around in my front room.

We look the following morning to see what time we got home via the tracker: 22:22. A sign. They are my 'angel numbers'. I think that Jake's maybe wishing me a happy birthday.

Polly, Charley, Louise and I are off to 30 East Drive. This is in Yorkshire and Charley is driving.

Number 30 East Drive is a haunted house and we are staying over doing séances etc. Love this shit.

I already know this will be hilarious as Charley and I have form on road trips.

Me and Polly catch a train to Charley's and she picks us up twenty minutes late from the station. She announces she will need petrol soon. Instead of heading for the nearest petrol station, which is literally round the corner, she decides to drive about twenty-five miles away and we end up not far from where Polly and I started our journey. For fuck's sake.

It has begun.

We stock up on snacks for the journey as well as petrol. We're off.

We basically chain smoke (car is like a scene out of *Cheech and Chong*) and listen to an eclectic mix of our fave songs.

We stop for a coffee once we hit the 'WELCOME TO THE NORTH' sign, smoke a bit more and go for a wee.

I've noticed once I'm in the service bathroom that my eyelashes (false) have started to detach. I would imagine this is due to the fact our windows have been opened doing eighty on the motorway!

They are swiftly peeled off and discarded like little spiders. I take my make up off as well because my eyes are itchy from the smoke and dust. Clearly, I'm looking sensational but other than demons, I've got nobody to impress this evening.

It takes us around four hours to get to our destination. We're all hyper with excitement!

We almost wet ourselves when we finally see the street sign of East Drive. It is not what I expected at all. It's on an estate and the house looks like your normal run of the mill seventies semi.

We grab our shit from the boot as we're staying the night (as you do) and head to the house.

We're greeted but a woman who looks like she's half demonic. She's got weird eyes and long, long black hair. She greets us with a friendly Mancunian accent and immediately looks less demonic. She tells us the rules and shows us where we can smoke (frankly, I'm done with the cigs and actually go and brush my teeth in this pit of a downstairs bathroom). She lets us know there's just one other group with us this evening.

She shows us around and it really is just like your nan's seventies semi including garish carpet and wallpaper. The other group arrive. They're much younger than us: a brother and sister and her best friend, but they seem positive. There's nothing worse than attending these things with people who don't believe. It really spoils it.

It's a brilliant night. Loads of screaming and running away, particularly me and Polly.

Charley decides at around 5 a.m. — bear in mind we've not slept at all — to drive back home straight away. That journey was looong. I felt so bad for Charley as she did all the driving but we kept stopping where we could so we could stretch our legs and get fresh air.

Finally, we get home. We're exhausted but it was well worth it.

My step-daughter posts something on Facebook this morning. It's basically about her having a headache and that if she dies, it may have been an aneurysm with lots of laughing out loud emojis.

I literally want to punch her in the fanny.

Some people are so insensitive. But I go on to over-analyse it. Maybe it's me being over sensitive?

July 2021

Off to Sheffield today with Isla (who lost her husband too). We both got their names engraved on the Heart of Steel — a memorial situated in Meadowhall Shopping Centre. It's finally open to the public after lockdown.

Our road trip was pretty good and uneventful. I think both of us, although we want to see this, are filled with a bit of anxiety as to how it may make us feel.

Anyhoo, we get there and go straight to the shopping centre to have a look.

It's bigger than I thought and the engravings in comparison are tiny but we locate them and take pictures.

It's emotional but also nice to see that they're always going to be on that heart.

We decide to go for lunch (with a cocktail) before we check into our hotel. We chill out for a bit, have a little drinkie and then try to find the hotel.

Now, I know I have form with road trips but hear me out. It took us approximately four hours to make the journey without any issues at all. We ask a couple of people for directions to the Premier Inn and get told it is a ten-minute walk away which is fine. We attempt to jump in a cab but after fifteen minutes or so, we decide to try to set out on foot. We're in the car park of the shopping centre. I shit you not, it takes us the best part of a fucking hour to navigate out of the car park onto a death trap crossing (with luggage) before we spot the purple haven that is the Premier Inn. It was literally across the road. FML.

We check in and as it's now approaching 6 p.m., we decide to quickly get changed and then I will go call for Isla in her room. It's like I am back in junior school.

We pop down to the bar, which is quite nice, and order a gigantic glass of red which is delicious and then grab a taxi into the centre. We get stopped by a slightly inebriated homeless chap and as he's caught me off guard and slightly tipsy, he gets a fiver.

Isla booked us a table in Yates for drinks and dinner. I do not know what we were thinking as it's an absolute dive. But on the plus side, they have twin toilets so you can pee with a mate. Obviously, we take advantage of that.

We find Turtle Bay, grab a burger and some cocktails and then head back to the hotel bar.

It's fairly quiet. We order the obligatory giant glass of wine for each of us. There's a chap sitting behind us on his own and we ask him if he can watch our drinks while we pop out for a cig. He tells us it's a disgusting habit (he's smiling though) and says he will.

Now before you all get on your high horses about leaving your drinks with a stranger in a place you don't know, I know it's irresponsible, but my mindset is continually switched to 'reckless'.

Anyway, he hasn't drugged us and he makes small talk telling us he's an ice cream man. Goals. For some reason, he ends up holding my hand. Probably feels sorry for me as we've told him our widow stories and he's kind of stroking my hand. I am so fucking uncomfortable at this stage and I need to make an exit.

I make an excuse to pop out for a cig and tell Isla we need to get away as he's full on. She agrees and peace is restored. We sneak back in avoiding the bar and find a vending machine on the way. Snacks: Mini Cheddars and a giant Twix plus obligatory diet coke are purchased for midnight snackage.

The next morning, we see the ice cream man checking out of the hotel with a wife and brood of kids. Men. Uneventful journey home and relieved to get back to my little sanctuary.

August 2021

Off to Greg and Natalie's with the folks and Polly today.

Mother's already stressing me out, telling me my directions are wrong. Anyway, we get there and start on the café tequila, obviously.

Both Greg and Natalie are on form. However, Polly and I plus Mother are getting exceedingly drunker by the second. We're sat in their summer house in the garden and we're chatting about last month's visit to Sheffield and I say to Mum, 'Did you like the pics I sent?'

She responds with, 'They're not the best of you.'

Polly is enraged which transpires into a row between the pair of them and although I completely agree with Polly, I cannot row with my mum. It makes me so anxious it's untrue. She's one of the only people I have to bite my tongue for. She's got a knack of making me feel guilty if I have an opinion.

Calm is eventually restored as Greg rolls a big fat spliff and gives it to Mum. I realise my family are one of a kind. I have a little dance with my dad which is cute.

Once the olds fuck off, we all start on the red wine bar. Polly sticks to her beloved tinnies and eventually I pass out on their sofa and Polly calls a taxi and we go back to mine.

Don't recall anything after that.

Next morning, I appear to have lost a shoe. Cinder fucking rella me.

I forgot I broke my toe that day and clearly decided I could only dance around in one shoe.

I'm out with Trixie today for a day drinking session.

We have a blast. She bollocks me though as I heckle with a 'drunk' in the high street who says we looks like mother and daughter. Rude bitch.

We end the night on a large Baileys and go to bed fairly soberish. I wake up feeling okay, a far cry from most of my weekend antics. It's because Trixie keeps me in check and looks after me.

October 2021

Polly and I have booked a lodge not too far away with a hot tub for the weekend.

I'm still a bit weird about staying anywhere other than home out of choice. But I know it'll be a good weekend.

The lodge is stunning. I could fit my little place in it about four times. We clearly crack open the booze as soon as we get there. Polly has ordered an afternoon tea for us. Absolute rip off but, to be honest, the cakes are worth it.

As soon as it gets dark, we get kitted up in bikinis and hit the hot tub. It's absolute bliss. We've got tunes being played on my phone and a little cool box with booze a plenty.

After a while, we run out of booze so I get out of the hot tub to refill the cool box, forgetting that it is fucking October, about 9 p.m. and freezing after spending three hours in ninety degree water. Polly is pissing herself as apparently there is steam coming off me.

I leg it back almost colliding with the glass doors and hot foot it back into the tub.

We get kicked out of the hot tub at about 11 p.m. by a man with a torch as you're not allowed in it after 10 p.m. We comply.

Next day, we are hanging out of our arses and chill out as it is pissing down. We try to do a ouija board but nothing happens. We order a curry which takes about two hours to turn up and by then, we could practically eat our own legs.

✳✳✳

Me and Polly are off on another ghost adventure. This time to Liverpool. Some gigantic mental asylum/orphanage. Nice.

We are training it as neither of us drive. It's an easy journey to Euston. Everything has been prebooked so all tickets are bought and with us. We spot our platform and head off there to wait for the train. It is strangely quiet on the platform and although there are plenty of people disembarking the train, absolutely no one is trying to get on our train.

We go and find out seats and settle down with our snacks for the journey. Ten minutes pass and apart from a cleaner, no one else is on the train. Polly suddenly says, 'East Kilbride sounds a bit Scotlandy,' after watching the stopping points the train is due at. We run off said train.

It transpires in Euston Station there are separate platforms for departures and arrivals. We were on arrivals.

We go to the ticket office. We have to rebook our tickets as we've missed our actual scheduled train.

Another sixty quid and we wait an hour for the next train.

This turns up with no incident but because we haven't prebooked this one, there are no seats available. After about thirty minutes, we find a couple of vacant seats and settle down for another few hours.

Liverpool is crazy. We check in to our hotel which is pretty cool and very, very old.

We have a few hours to kill before we set off at 9 p.m., so we grab a McDonalds, of course, and have a little nana nap before getting changed and grabbing a cab to the venue.

Another brilliant few hours and we end up getting a cab around 3 a.m. back to the hotel. We are both starving and thirsty and to our utter amazement, Liverpool is still kicking and we find a little shop and grab some diet coke, biscuits and crisps!

November 2021

I feel I need a bloody good old cry today so I open YouTube and listen to every motherfucking song that reminds me of Jake. Do you know what though? Although I'm crying, it's a kind of relieved happy cry. I feel connected with him and know he's looking down on me probably laughing his tits off at me for being such a sop.

December 2021

Me and the sister are out with Jake's nieces this evening in London.

There's a chap at the station who can barely stand. He manages to kind of fall into a display unit and there is an almighty crash and he's flat out. A couple of staff check on him and escort him into the main station area. They prop him up and he's very bleary eyed. He's not a bad looking chap. About forty-five, all suited and booted, and doesn't look the sort to get completely clattered. We go over to him to make sure he's okay and can get home. Bless him, I think it must've scared him as he's much more compos mentis. We tell him we've all been there and that it's likely we will be in a worse state later.

At Waterloo Station, both girls are on form as usual. We get there before them and before you know it, we can hear Sienna shouting, 'Auntie Simone, Auntie Polly,' at the top of her voice and then we run to each other. You can tell immediately what kind of evening this will be.

Sienna is already completely mashed, but hilarious.

We get a cab to Covent Garden and find a nice pub. It's busy but we find a seat for all four of us.

Me and Polly go to the bar and stand there for a minute

or so just chatting shit waiting to be served.

I really don't know how to explain this without expressing it on my face, but I'm going to try. There was a barman standing slightly away from where we were waiting. He was kind of one of those Viking looking blokes. He didn't speak or smile, he just held our eye contact and kind of moved his eyeballs only in a downwards position. After a minute or two, we finally clocked that where we were both standing there was a sign that clearly said: you will not be served here, please move down the bar.

We moved further down the bar obviously laughing hysterically and as soon as we were in the correct vicinity, the barman's whole persona completely changed and he was friendly and chatty and immediately took our drinks order.

I suppose you had to be there but I swear we could barely string a sentence together we were laughing too much.

Eventually, we leave to go to another venue. Polly stacks it on the way and we decide maybe it's time we leave.

We celebrate another Jake day a week or so later with Polly with two tattoos and red wine and tapas. Perfect.

Epilogue

I started writing this around a year after he died.

The first three or four months were just a blur. I would have happily ended my life during the initial stages. I think I've aged my sister by about ten years. I didn't care about me and didn't realise how much pain I may have caused my nearest and dearest should I have actually gone through with it.

I can say though that it does get easier. The sharp edges that stick you in the guts on a daily basis do get softer.

Almost three years on, I have realised I don't cry anymore. I want to cry, but the tears don't come. The knot in my stomach and chest comes and goes.

In the beginning, the worst thing was waking up and, as cliché as it seems, you do actually, for a nano-second, forget. But then there is that empty space and you realise it isn't just a nightmare. That was the hardest moment to deal with.

Or seeing someone who bears a vague resemblance to him, maybe wearing the same coat or walking in a familiar way. Your mind so wants it to be them but then you see that it's not. That's hard too.

The memories make me smile but there is always an

underlying sadness that comes alongside it whenever I am looking at his pictures or thinking about him.

Is it normal not to cry? The guilt of not being able to cry is strong. Does it mean I don't give a shit anymore? Have I got used to being without him?

What is normal though? Why do I put myself through this guilt? Would he want me to cry? I know the answer but still it feels wrong.

The tablets I am on have stabilised me. The PTSD resulting from the trauma of the resuscitation has dissipated, and I suppose that's the point of taking them.

They seem to have compartmentalised the irrational thoughts of not wanting to go on without him in my life; they have been boxed up and packaged deep inside of my head, like a little parcel or maybe a ticking time bomb.

I looked up not being able to cry on the internet. Apparently, it is a common 'side effect' of some anti-depressants, and it is called emotional blunting.

The sadness hasn't completely gone. Sometimes when I'm listening to a song and the lyrics seem to be made for how I feel, the feeling of uncontrollable emotion comes out to play like a big fat slap in the fucking face but my life is bearable. Or I have a day where I just feel a bit low. Usually this comes after having a really good weekend. It's almost like a come down but without the drugs, then anything can tip me over the edge and I can end up like a blubbering wreck.

The thoughts can be so debilitating and can take me to a bad place again, but these moments are less and less.

People can be critical of suicide. The usual response is: what a selfish thing to do. If I'm honest, I was one of those people before what happened happened.

But unless you've been in a place so dark and your heart has completely cracked into tiny little pieces, or you feel you've nowhere left to go, then frankly you should really button it.

Maybe my own suicidal thoughts could be perceived as selfish but I honestly didn't want to live without him.

This is the only reason I carry on taking the happy pills. I don't want to go back to that dark, dark place. I want to be able to go on.

Sometimes out of the blue, I am hit with the enormity of what has happened and that he really isn't coming back. It can be the most mundane of scenarios that can trigger a 'temporary relapse' like watching a programme on TV and not understanding the storyline and not being able to ask him to explain it to me (this happened frequently when he was still here, brain of a small Shetland rabbit) or being in a place we often went to and looking for him… and he's simply not there.

Most of all, I miss laughing with him. We always laughed together. He'd make me belly laugh and we just got each other.

I didn't ever think my new life without him would

be bearable. The hang-ups when dialling 116 123 (if you know, you know), the bottles of wine sunk in despair, and the sobbing down the phone to my sister have subsided. However, it doesn't mean I love him any less. But I have realised I don't want to die. I just want the pain to stop.

I work so hard to keep his memory alive by talking about him constantly. I want others to talk about him, and I want to believe he is here with me.

You also have to appreciate that others may react in a completely different way. His son just withdrew and found it hard to face up to, my parents were satisfied that I was okay so it was almost swept under the rug. Life goes on for most but when you're hit with the love of your life going unexpectedly, it seems so unfair that others just get on with their lives. You're struck with the utter unfairness of it all.

Covid sadly helped me. I am deeply sorry for anyone who lost loved ones during this shit storm but having everyone else locked down and not being able to get on with 'life as normal' made it slightly easier for me.

I suppose what I am trying to get across is that however you feel, whether you have been through something similar or are going through a tremendous amount of pressure from illness, grief or anything else that has affected your well-being, anything goes.

However you feel, it's okay. The pain might never disappear or it might, either way that's okay.

I have realised through all of this that it is okay to be

selfish. In fact, I would say it is imperative. I don't have enough love, patience or sanity left in me to help others. In my opinion, you really do need to be number one. That probably sounds cruel but I need to be honest in how I feel.

I expressed this to my sister as I thought that maybe some people may think I am a bit of a cold fish, but she said that I hide it well. Outwardly, I am the same generous, laugh a minute, happy go fucking lucky girl, but inwardly, I want to stab people in the eye. Some people.

Having the right people around you is so important but equally so is being on your own. This is just my own opinion and I'd never judge anyone for feeling any different. Grief is so multifaceted. There is no right or wrong way to feel.

Up until very recently, I probably would silently judge somebody who has 'moved on'. I shouldn't. That's not fair. I should be saying, 'Good for them.'

A couple of weeks ago, I had my first 'sexual' encounter with another man. To be honest, I was absolutely clattered but he was also a 'snack' which was a bonus. It was a lustful session and we almost went all the way but didn't.

The following days I have never felt so bloody guilty for this incident. It didn't help that it mainly occurred in my front room and Jake's cushions and pictures are everywhere. It must've been so inviting for this poor guy. I didn't eat for a day (unheard of) and was constantly apologising to Jake.

Then I started to feel resentment towards him, which

I hadn't experienced before. I found myself saying to him that it was his fault as he had left me so I was entitled to get fruity with someone else. It was like I was justifying myself. I felt an odd mixture of extreme guilt crossed with the excitement of feeling desirable again.

To be honest, it really fucked with my head.

So, who knows what's round the corner. I'll just keep trying to move forwards at my own pace. I think I'll have to write a chapter of 'Life After'!

I know others who have lost loved ones and have gone on to do charity events and other events to maybe raise money etc. I just feel guilty because I can't do that. I honour him by getting drunk at least three times a year in memory of him. That's about my limit, not fucking bungee jumping off of a mountain top. I am amazed how selfless some can be when dealing with grief. I think I have become quite selfish but hey ho, you've got to do whatever you can to get through the dark days.

I am a harsh critic of both myself and how I have handled this whole sorry situation, but if I look back maybe I should give myself a pat on the back as I have come through what I sincerely hope is the worst experience I ever have to go through.

I wish he was still here. I have had to deal with eight-legged horses on my own, but I am now a small size 12. I call it the heartbreak diet. Always got to look on the bright side and try to be a Positive Patsy.

Update: August 2022

So far this year, I have fractured my wrist in a non-alcohol related incident involving a long dress and DMs, ended up being wheeled up to a drive-through McDonalds in a shopping trolley, watched *365 Days* and because of this, joined a BDSM 'dating' site and met a Daddy.

Maybe there should be a

Part 2?

Watch this space.

Printed in Great Britain
by Amazon